Focus on Grammar

WORKBOOK

A
BASIC
Course for
Reference
and Practice

A
BASIC
Course for
Reference
and Practice

Samuela Eckstut

Longman

Focus on Grammar: A Basic Course for Reference and Practice Workbook

Addison-Wesley, 10 Bank Street, White Plains, NY 10606

Editorial Director: Joanne Dresner
Development Editor: Joan Saslow
Production Editorial: Lisa A. Hutchins, Helen B. Ambrosio
Text design and production: Six West Design
Cover design: A Good Thing, Inc.
Text art: Marie DeJohn
Cartoons: Dahlia Schoenberg

ISBN 0-201-65683-3

3 4 5 6 7 8 9 10-CRS-99 98 97 96 95

Contents

Unit 1 Present Tense of *Be* 1

Unit 2 Nouns, Adjectives, and Prepositions 13

Unit 3 *Wh-* Questions; Possessive Nouns; Prepositions of Time and Place 26

Unit 4 Imperatives; *There is/There are* 40

Uni 5 Present Progressive 58

Unit 6 Simple Present Tense 70

Unit 7 Simple Present Tense and Present Progressive 84

Unit 8 Simple Past Tense 97

Unit 9 Past Tense of *Be* 114

Unit 10 Nouns and Quantifiers; Modals: *Can, Could, Would* 127

Unit 11 Future; Modals: *May* and *Might* 149

Unit 12 Comparisons 166

Unit 13 Past Progressive; Direct and Indirect Objects 185

Unit 14 Modals: *Should, Had better, Have to; Must;* Superlatives 202

Putting It All Together 218

Answer Key 226

About the Author

Samuela Eckstut has taught ESL and EFL for eighteen years, in the United States and in Greece, Italy, and England. Currently she is teaching at Boston University, Center for English Language and Orientation Programs (CELOP). She has authored or co-authored numerous texts for the teaching of English, notably *What's in a Word? Reading and Vocabulary Building, In the Real World, Interlink, First Impressions, Beneath the Surface,* and *Widely Read.*

UNIT 1

Present Tense of Be

A AFFIRMATIVE STATEMENTS WITH *BE*

A.1

Complete the conversations. Use **I am, you are, he is, she is, it is, we are,** *or* **they are.**

1. **A:** How are you?

   B: *I am* fine.

2. **A:** How are you and your wife?

   B: ______________ fine.

3. **A:** How is your daughter?

   B: ______________ fine.

4. **A:** How is your son?

   B: ______________ fine.

5. **A:** How are your mother and father?

   B: ______________ fine.

6. **A:** Where are you?

   B: ______________ in the garden.

7. **A:** Where is the sandwich?

   B: ______________ on the table.

8. **A:** Where are the keys?

   B: ______________ in the car.

9. **A:** Where is Mrs. Robinson?

   B: ______________ in the office.

10. **A:** Where am I?

    B: ______________ here.

A.2

Change the underlined words. Use **he, she, it, we,** *or* **they.**

Hello. I am Rocco. My last name is Marciano. ~~My last name~~ *It* (1.) is an Italian name. My family and I (2.) are from Italy. Anna is my mother. My mother (3.) is from a village in Abruzzi. The village (4.) is very small. Silvano is my father. My father (5.) is from Naples. Naples (6.) is a big city in the south of Italy. I am from Naples, too.

My parents are in Italy now. My parents (7.) are on vacation. I am at home with my sisters. My sisters and I (8.) are not happy alone. My sisters (9.) are always angry with me. My brother is lucky. My brother (10.) is not at home. My brother (11.) is at college. The college (12.) is far away.

A.3

Write true statements. Use words from columns **A, B,** *and* **C** *in each sentence.*

A	B	C
I		at home
My best friend		at work
My mother	am	cold
My father	is	happy
My teacher	are	heavy
My parents		hot
My classmates		late
		short
		tall
		thin
		worried
		a student
		a nice person
		nice people

1. ______________________________ 4. ______________________________

2. ______________________________ 5. ______________________________

3. ______________________________ 6. ______________________________

7. ______________________ 9. ______________________

8. ______________________ 10. ______________________

B CONTRACTIONS OF AFFIRMATIVE STATEMENTS WITH *BE*

B.1

Write the dialogues in full form.

1. **A:** It's eight o'clock. *It is eight o'clock.*
   B: Oh, no! We're late. *Oh, no! We are late.*
2. **A:** We're here. ______________________
   B: That's wonderful. ______________________
3. **A:** Your food's on the table. ______________________
   B: Good! I'm hungry. ______________________
4. **A:** Charlie's in love with Linda. ______________________
   B: But she's married! ______________________
5. **A:** I'm sorry about the window. ______________________
   B: That's okay. ______________________
6. **A:** I think the picture's beautiful. ______________________
   B: You're crazy. It's terrible. ______________________
7. **A:** I'm so glad to be here. ______________________
   B: We're glad, too. ______________________

B.2

Write the dialogues with contractions.

1. **A:** It is eight o'clock. *It's eight o'clock.*
   B: Oh, no! We are late. *Oh, no! We're late.*
2. **A:** That woman is beautiful. ______________________
   B: She is my wife. ______________________

(Continued on next page.)

3. **A:** Hello. I am Nancy Marks. ______________________

   B: Hi. My name is Hank Stewart. ______________________

4. **A:** They are nice people. ______________________

   B: But they are so boring. ______________________

5. **A:** My daughter is in the hospital. ______________________

   B: We are sorry to hear that. ______________________

6. **A:** We are glad to meet you. ______________________

   B: It is nice to meet you, too. ______________________

7. **A:** My boyfriend is fifty-five years old. ______________________

   B: But you are only twenty. ______________________

C NEGATIVE STATEMENTS AND CONTRACTIONS WITH *BE*

C.1

Look at the picture. Put a check (✓) next to the sentences that are correct. Change the sentences that are wrong.

1. The women are middle-aged. *The women are not middle-aged.*
2. Two women are with a man. ______________________

3. The people are in a house. ____________________
4. A dog is with three people. ____________________
5. The dog is black. ____________________
6. The man is fat. ____________________
7. The women are sisters. ____________________
8. It is cold. ____________________
9. The women are thin. ____________________
10. I am in the picture. ____________________

C.2

Correct the sentences.

1. Dallas is a state.

   Dallas is not a state. It is a city.

2. California is a country.

   ____

3. Russia is small.

   ____

4. Egypt and China are people.

   ____

5. Boston and New York are in Canada.

   ____

6. Miami is a state.

   ____

7. Toronto is in the United States.

   ____

8. Toyotas and Fords are airplanes.

   ____

(Continued on next page.)

9. New York is the capital of the United States.

____

10. Cigarettes are good for people.

____

11. The sun and the moon are near Earth.

____

C.3

Complete the sentences. Use **is, is not, are,** *or* **are not.**

1. Apples *are not* black.
2. The Earth ____________ round.
3. The sun ____________ cold.
4. Ice cream and chocolate ____________ good for you.
5. Lemons ____________ yellow.
6. Cars ____________ cheap.
7. Peter ____________ a name.
8. An elephant ____________ a small animal.
9. English, Spanish, and Arabic ____________ languages.
10. The president of the United States ____________ a doctor.

C.4

Write the dialogues in full form.

1. **A:** Carol's angry with her father. — *Carol is angry with her father.*

   B: I'm not surprised. — *I am not surprised.*

2. **A:** I'm right. ____________

   B: No, you aren't. You're wrong. ____________

3. **A:** Mrs. Morris isn't well. ____________

   B: I know. Her daughter's worried about her. ____________

4. **A:** It's time for bed. ______________________________

   B: But I'm not tired. ______________________________

5. **A:** They're my books. ______________________________

   B: No, they're not. They're my books. ______________________________

6. **A:** My keys aren't here. ______________________________

   B: They're in my bag. ______________________________

7. **A:** Maria and Ali aren't in class today. ______________________________

   B: They're lucky. ______________________________

C.5

Write the dialogues with contractions.

1. **A:** Carol is angry with her father. *Carol's angry with her father.*

   B: I am not surprised. *I'm not surprised.*

2. **A:** I am afraid. ______________________________

   B: Why? The dog is not dangerous. ______________________________

3. **A:** The taxi is here. ______________________________

   B: But I am not ready. ______________________________

4. **A:** You are not from the hospital. ______________________________

   B: No, we are police officers. ______________________________

5. **A:** They are not bad children. ______________________________

   B: No, but they are bad students. ______________________________

6. **A:** Your bag is on the table. ______________________________

   B: It is not my bag. ______________________________

7. **A:** This gift is for you. ______________________________

   B: But it is not my birthday. ______________________________

D *YES/NO* QUESTIONS AND SHORT ANSWERS

D.1

Put a question mark (?) at the end of each question. Put a period (.) at the end of each sentence.

Examples: Milt Singer is a detective.

Is Milt Singer a detective?

1. Are you Rocky
2. Are you and your classmates worried
3. Is your teacher in school today
4. We are very good students
5. I am very thirsty
6. Is the dog hungry
7. Oregon is near Canada
8. Are the children afraid of the dog
9. Is your car red
10. This exercise is easy

D.2

Match the questions and answers.

1. __*d*__ Is Preeda from Thailand?	a. Yes, she is. She's in the kitchen with my father.
2. ______ Are Pat and Tom American?	b. Yes, we are. Our teacher's wonderful.

3. ______ Are you Lucy Simone?
4. ______ Are you ready?
5. ______ Is the doctor in the office?
6. ______ Are Mr. and Mrs. Saris here?
7. ______ Is the TV in the living room?
8. ______ Is John married?
9. ______ Is the book good?
10. ______ Are you students at King High School?
11. ______ Is your mother home?
12. ______ Are you and the other students happy in this class?

c. Yes, they're in the garden.
d. Yes, he is. He's from Bangkok.
e. No, we're students at Kennedy High School.
f. No, they're not. They're British.
g. No, it isn't. It's in the bedroom.
h. No, I'm Anna Sanchez.
i. Yes, it is. It's very interesting.
j. No, I'm not. Please wait a minute.
k. Yes, he is. His wife's a detective.
l. No, she isn't. She's at the hospital.

D.3

Write questions.

1. Milt singer/you/are

   Are you Milt Singer?
2. you/are/happy

   ____
3. a student/your mother/is

   ____
4. clean/is/your bedroom

   ____
5. are/from Texas/your friends

   ____
6. Carol Winston/your friend/is

   ____

(Continued on next page.)

7. a detective/are/you

____

8. your teacher/is/friendly

____

9. your mother and father/Canadian/are

____

10. are/in love/you

____

11. middle aged/your classmates/are

____

D.4

Answer the questions in exercise D.3. Use short answers.

1. (Are you Milt Singer?)

   No, I'm not.

2. _______________
3. _______________
4. _______________
5. _______________
6. _______________
7. _______________
8. _______________
9. _______________
10. _______________
11. _______________

E IT'S + TIME

E.1

Look at the map and answer the questions.

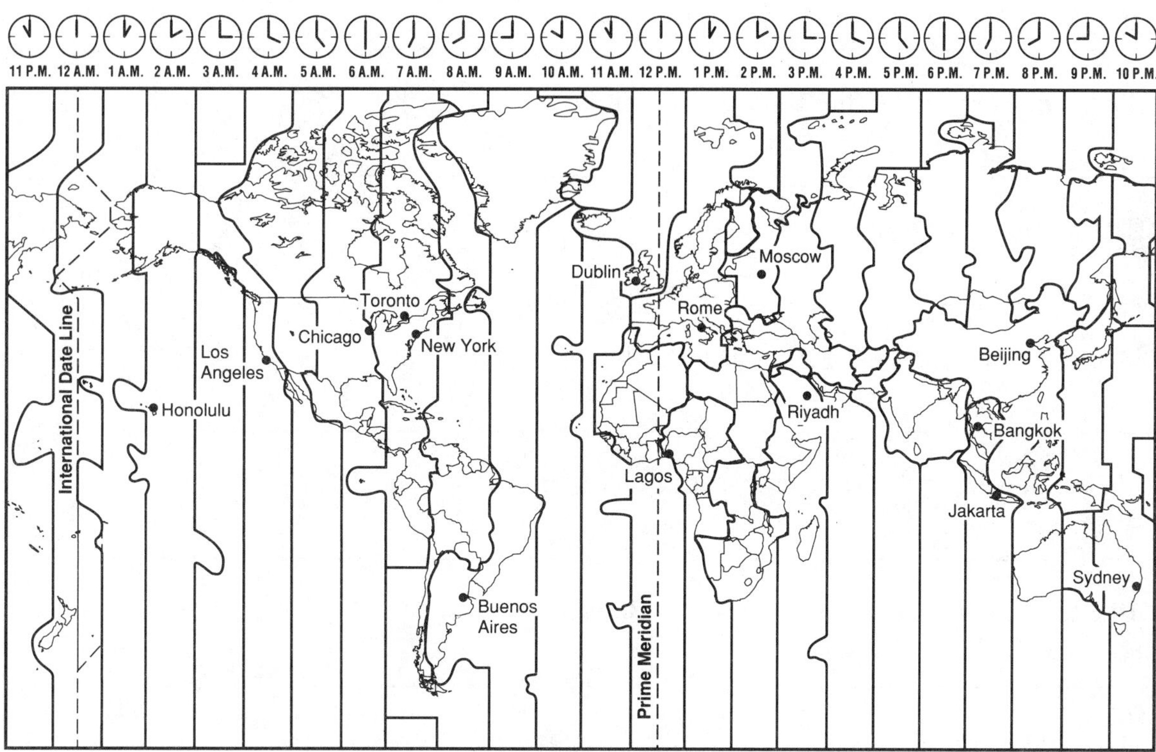

1. It's 11:30 P.M. in New York. What time is it in Chicago?

   It's half past ten. ________ OR *It's ten-thirty.* ________

2. It's 10:15 P.M. in New York. What time is it in Honolulu?

   ________________ OR ________________

3. It's 12:55 A.M. in New York. What time is it in Beijing?

   ________________ OR ________________

4. It's 4:00 P.M. in New York. What time is it in Lagos?

   ________________ OR ________________

5. It's 9:30 P.M. in New York. What time is it in Toronto?

   ________________ OR ________________

(Continued on next page.)

6. It's 1:45 A.M. in New York. What time is it in Jakarta?

______________________ OR ______________________

7. It's 5:50 P.M. in New York. What time is it in Buenos Aires?

______________________ OR ______________________

8. It's 8:25 A.M. in New York. What time is it in Sydney?

______________________ OR ______________________

9. It's 6:40 P.M. in New York. What time is it in Dublin?

______________________ OR ______________________

10. It's 11:20 A.M. in New York. What time is it in Moscow?

______________________ OR ______________________

11. It's 3:05 P.M. in New York. What time is it in Riyadh?

______________________ OR ______________________

12. It's 7:35 A.M. in New York. What time is it in Los Angeles?

______________________ OR ______________________

13. It's 2:10 A.M. in New York. What time is it in Bangkok?

______________________ OR ______________________

UNIT

Nouns, Adjectives, and Prepositions

A COUNT NOUNS; A/AN

A.1

Match the people with their occupations.

1. __e__ Péle
2. ____ Dustin Hoffman
3. ____ Elizabeth II
4. ____ Madonna
5. ____ Neil Armstrong
6. ____ Mikhail Gorbachev
7. ____ Yo Yo Ma
8. ____ Kristi Yamaguchi
9. ____ Jodie Foster

a. actor
b. ice skater
c. musician
d. former political leader
e. soccer player
f. queen
g. astronaut
h. actress
i. singer

A.2

Write sentences about the people in exercise A.1.

1. *Péle is a soccer player.*
2. ____
3. ____
4. ____
5. ____
6. ____
7. ____
8. ____
9. ____

A.3

Say these plural nouns. Then write them in the correct columns.

actresses
boxes
boys
carrots
classes
dictionaries
girls
houses
lemons
roommates
sons
states
students
watches

/z/	/ɪz/	/s/
boys	*actresses*	*carrots*

A.4

Complete the sentences. Use the plural form of the words in the box.

actress	country	river	university
car	man	song	watch
city	mountain	state	woman
continent	province		

1. Toyotas and Fords are *cars*.
2. Mrs. Robb and Ms. Hernandez are __________.
3. Mr. Katz and John Mallin are __________.
4. "Jingle Bells" and "Happy Birthday to You" are __________.
5. London and Cairo are __________.
6. The Nile and the Amazon are __________.
7. Asia and Africa are __________.
8. Florida and Michigan are __________.
9. Brazil and Kenya are __________.
10. Ontario and Quebec are __________.
11. Harvard and Yale are __________.
12. Seikos and Rolexes are __________.
13. Demi Moore and Julia Roberts are __________.
14. The Himalayas and the Alps are __________.

A.5

Write the singular or plural form of the nouns.

1. 4 women
   \+ 1 *woman*
   5 *women*

2. 1 child
   \+ 2 ________
   3 ________

3. 1 tooth
   \+ 6 ________
   7 ________

4. 3 feet
   \+ 1 ________
   4 ________

5. 6 grandchildren
   \+ 1 ________
   7 ________

6. 8 people
   \+ 1 ________
   9 ________

7. 1 sister-in-law
   \+ 2 ________
   3 feet

A.6

Unscramble the word and write a sentence. Use **it's** *or* **they're.**

1. edb — *It's a bed.*
2. vnsiek — *They're knives.*
3. veno ________
4. usheo ________
5. kobos ________
6. genora ________
7. seey ________
8. esxbo ________
9. ooattp ________

(Continued on next page.)

10. geg ____________________

11. pleap ____________________

12. chatw ____________________

B DESCRIPTIVE ADJECTIVES

B.1

Write the opposites of the underlined words.

1. **A:** Is the man <u>tall</u>?

   B: Yes, but his sons are ___short___.

2. **A:** Is your dog <u>small</u>?

   B: Yes, but the other dogs are ____________________.

3. **A:** Is the book <u>interesting</u>?

   B: Yes, but the movie is ____________________.

4. **A:** Is Bertha <u>thin</u>?

   B: Yes, but her daughter is ____________________.

5. **A:** Is this watch <u>cheap</u>?

   B: Yes, but the other watches are ____________________.

6. **A:** Is your room <u>clean</u>?

   B: Yes, but the other rooms are ____________________.

7. **A:** Is the little girl <u>quiet</u>?

   B: Yes, but the little boys are ____________________.

8. **A:** Are the students <u>good</u>?

   B: Yes, but one student is ____________________.

9. **A:** Are your shoes <u>old</u>?

   B: Yes, but the other shoes are ________________.

10. **A:** Are your feet <u>hot</u>?

    B: Yes, but my hands are ________________.

B.2

Find the mistake. Then write the correct sentence.

1. The olds shoes are over there.

   The old shoes are over there.

2. They are men honest.

   ____

3. They are talls girls.

   ____

4. They are animals intelligent.

   ____

5. Those books are expensives.

   ____

6. Eggs are whites or browns.

   ____

7. They are actors good.

   ____

8. These watches are cheaps.

   ____

9. They are stories interesting.

   ____

B.3

Write one sentence from the two sentences.

1. You are boys. You are bad.

   You are bad boys.

2. It is a book. It is great.

3. Bill Clinton is a politican. Bill Clinton is famous.

4. She is a singer. She is beautiful.

5. They are students. They are intelligent.

6. He is a man. He is nice.

7. They are cameras. They are expensive.

8. It is a story. It is long.

9. We are doctors. We are good.

10. You are a woman. You are lucky.

C POSSESSIVE ADJECTIVES

C.1

Match the questions and answers.

1. __c__ Is John your son?
2. ______ Is your home on this street?
3. ______ Is he Joe and Karen's son?
4. ______ Is Ms. Turner's home near here?
5. ______ Is she a famous actress?
6. ______ Are they rich?
7. ______ Is Tom Wong a doctor?
8. ______ Is that man your friend?
9. ______ Is our table ready?

a. No, their son is not here.
b. No, but her office is.
c. No, Mark is my son.
d. Yes, it is. Please come with me.
e. No, we are not from here.
f. No, her sister is.
g. No, his daughter is.
h. Yes, his name is Sam Miller.
i. No, but their friends are.

C.2

Complete the conversations. Use **my, your, his, her, our,** *or* **their.**

1. **Jack:** Is that my car?

   Jill: No, _____your_____ car isn't here.

2. **Ms. Bou:** Jim, is this __________________ bag?

   Jim: No, it isn't.

   Ms. Bou: Is it Sue and Harry's bag?

   Jim: No, __________________ bag is over there.

3. **Mr. Miller:** Is this Mrs. Waller's box?

   Barbara: No, that's __________________ box.

   Mr. Miller: Is it Mr. Luca's box?

   Barbara: Maybe it's __________________ box. I'm not sure.

(Continued on next page.)

4. **Mrs. Carter:** Is this your family's dog?

Ben: No, ____________________ dog is black.

Mrs. Carter: Is it Mr. and Mrs. Haley's dog?

Ben: No, ____________________ dog is white.

5. **Alan:** Is this your office?

Ron: No, ____________________ office is on the second floor.

Alan: Is it Norma's office?

Ron: No, ____________________ office is on the first floor.

6. **Becky:** Stella, is that ____________________ husband in the picture?

Stella: Yes, ____________________ name is Dan.

Becky: And who's this?

Stella: It's ____________________ daughter. ____________________ name is Marie.

C.3

Complete the sentences. Use a subject pronoun or a possessive adjective.

1. Hi. I'm Yoko. _____I_____ 'm from Japan. _____My_____ home is in Tokyo.
2. This is Doug. ____________________ 's in New York. ____________________ bedroom is always messy.
3. This is Carol. ____________________ 's in Oregon. Yoko is ____________________ roommate.
4. This is Pete, and this is Elenore. ____________________ 're married. ____________________ last name is Winston. This is ____________________ home. ____________________ 's beautiful.
5. Hello. I'm Bertha and this is Lulu. ____________________ 're friends. ____________________ homes are in Florida.
6. Hi. I'm Norma. ____________________ 'm not married, but ____________________ boyfriend is very handsome.
7. This is Milt Singer. ____________________ 's a detective. ____________________ office is on Woodcock Street.

8. My husband and I are happy to meet you. ________________ 're here on vacation.

   ________________ hotel is near the beach. ________________ name is the Grand Hotel.

   ________________ 's a very nice place.

9. These are our children. ________________ names are Katie and Chris. ________________ 're

   not at home this month. ________________ 're with my mother. ________________ 's not

   very lucky.

D THIS/THESE

D.1

Circle the right word.

1. These box are heavy.
   (boxes)
2. These person are my classmates.
   people
3. This map is of Canada.
   maps
4. These book are expensive.
   books
5. This ice cream cone is delicious.
   ice cream cones
6. This is my girlfriends.
   girlfriend
7. These are my cats.
   cat
8. These flowers are beautiful.
   flower
9. This exercises is easy.
   exercise
10. These are pencils.
    pencil

D.2

Complete the conversations. Use **this** *or* **these** *and* **is** *or* **are.**

1. **A:** ___These___ ___are___ my socks.

   B: No, they're not. ___These___ ___are___ your socks and ___this___ ___is___ your shirt.

2. **A:** __________ __________ a gift for you.

   B: Oh, thank you.

3. **A:** __________ hamburger __________ terrible.

   B: __________ potatoes __________ awful, too.

4. **A:** __________ television __________ heavy.

   B: __________ bookcase __________ heavy, too.

5. **A:** Brenda, __________ __________ Tim.

   B: Hi, Tim. It's nice to meet you.

6. **A:** __________ shoes __________ only $35.

   B: Really?

7. **A:** __________ __________ a great party.

   B: I know.

8. **A:** __________ __________ beautiful earrings.

   B: __________ bracelet __________ nice, too.

9. **A:** __________ cookies __________ for you.

   B: Gee, that's nice of you. Thanks.

10. **A:** __________ __________ my parents.

    B: Really? They're so young.

D.3

Write questions. Use **What's this?** *or* **What are these?**

1. **A:** *What are these?*

   B: They're trees.

2. **A:** ______________________________

   B: It's the sun.

3. **A:** ______________________________

   B: It's my dog.

4. **A:** ______________________________

   B: It's a car.

5. **A:** ______________________________

   B: They're my dolls.

6. **A:** ______________________________

   B: They're flowers.

7. **A:** ______________________________

   B: It's a chair.

8. **A:** ______________________________

   B: They're balls.

9. **A:** ______________________________

   B: They're birds.

10. **A:** ______________________________

    B: It's a house.

E PREPOSITIONS OF PLACE

E.1

Draw a picture of each sentence.

1. A cat is under a chair. ______________________

2. A dog is on a chair. ______________________

3. A ball is between a dog and a cat. ______________________

4. A man is behind a chair. ______________________

5. An apple is next to a banana. ______________________

6. A woman is behind a little girl. ______________________

7. A ball is under a car. ______________________

8. A bicycle is next to a house. ______________________

9. Ten flowers are between two trees. ______________________________

10. Two boxes are on a bed. ______________________________

E.2

Look at the map on page A4 of your grammar book. Complete the sentences. Use **near, between, next to,** *or* **in**.

1. Seattle is ____in____ Washington.
2. Saskatchewan is ______________ Manitoba and Alberta.
3. Pennsylvania is ______________ New Jersey.
4. Maine is ______________ Massachusetts.
5. Halifax is ______________ Nova Scotia.
6. Kansas is ______________ Arkansas and Iowa.
7. Indiana is ______________ Ohio and Illinois.
8. Prince Edward Island is ______________ Canada.
9. Missouri is ______________ Oregon.
10. Ottawa is ______________ Montreal.

UNIT

3

Wh- Questions; Possessive Nouns; Prepositions of Time and Place

A QUESTIONS WITH *WHO, WHAT,* AND *WHERE*

A.1

Write the correct question words. Use **who, what,** *or* **where.**

1. ___Who___? My mother
2. ___Where___? At home
3. ______________? My best friend
4. ______________? In Texas
5. ______________? On Park Street
6. ______________? A sandwich
7. ______________? Abraham Lincoln and John Kennedy
8. ______________? Venezuela
9. ______________? Shakespeare
10. ______________? Soccer and basketball
11. ______________? Under the bed
12. ______________? A bird

A.2

Write questions.

1. are/parents/where/your

   Where are your parents?

2. in/is/car/the/who

   Who is in the car?

3. what/you/good at/sports/are

   ____

4. from/where/they/are

   ____

5. in/who/your/the/garden/is/woman

____

6. Dallas/where/is

____

7. shoes/are/where/my

____

8. bag/is/the/what/in

____

9. post office/the/is/where

____

10. who/your/writer/favorite/is

____

11. the United States/who/two/presidents/are/famous/of

____

12. tree/what/that/the/is/in

____

A.3

Match the questions in exercise A.2 with the answers in exercise A.1.

1. *Where are your parents*? *At home.*
2. *Who is in the car*? *My mother.*
3. ___? ___
4. ___? ___
5. ___? ___
6. ___? ___
7. ___? ___
8. ___? ___
9. ___? ___
10. ___? ___

(Continued on next page.)

11. ______________________________? ______________________

12. ______________________________? ______________________

A.4

Complete the sentences. Use **who, what** *or* **where.**

Norma: ______________'s Doug?
1.

Dad: I don't know. ______________ time is it?
2.

Norma: It's 8:30.

Dad: Maybe he's at the movies. Why? ______________'s the problem?
3.

Norma: There's a phone call for him.

Dad: ______________'s on the phone?
4.

Norma: A girl.

Dad: ______________'s her name?
5.

Norma: Minjung.

Dad: ______________'s Minjung?
6.

Norma: Doug's girlfriend.

Dad: Doug's girlfriend?

Norma: Uh-huh.

Dad: Minjung's an unusual name. ______________'s she from?
7.

Norma: Dad, I don't know. She's not my girlfriend.

A.5

Write the questions. Use **who, what,** *or* **where.**

1. **A:** *Who's that?*

   B: It's one of the students in my English class.

2. **A:** ____

   B: The hospital? It's on Porter Street.

3. **A:** ______________________________

   B: I think your keys are on the TV.

4. **A:** ______________________________

   B: Room 203 . . . Room 203. I'm sorry. I don't know.

5. **A:** ______________________________

   B: Bill Cosby? He's an actor.

6. **A:** ______________________________

   B: Mikhail Gorbachev and Ronald Reagan are former political leaders.

7. **A:** ______________________________

   B: The people in front of the building? They're tourists from Brazil.

8. **A:** ______________________________

   B: Cadillacs are cars.

9. **A:** ______________________________

   B: It's my answering machine.

10. **A:** ______________________________

    B: The wastepaper basket is next to the desk.

B POSSESSIVE NOUNS AND QUESTIONS WITH *WHOSE*

B.1

Rewrite the sentences. Change the underlined words.

1. Pete Winston's a businessman.

   He's a businessman.

2. Pete Winston's wife's a writer.

   His wife's a writer.

3. Pedro's last name is Barba.

   ____

(Continued on next page.)

4. Pedro's a grandfather.

5. The girls are with their grandfather.

6. The girls' names are Lydia and Daphne.

7. Lydia's twelve years old.

8. Lydia's hair is long.

9. Pedro's dogs are always outside.

10. Pedro's with his dogs.

11. Daphne's eyes are blue.

12. Daphne's afraid of the dogs.

13. The dogs' food is in the garage.

14. The dogs are in the garage.

15. The children's friends are not with them today.

16. The children are happy to be with their grandfather.

B.2

Larry is at the store and has the wrong bag of food. Write questions. Use **whose**.

1. This is not my coffee.

   Whose coffee is it?

2. These are not my apples.

   Whose apples are they?

3. These are not my eggs.

   ____

4. These are not my bananas.

   ____

5. This is not my bread.

   ____

6. These are not my potatoes.

   ____

7. This is not my cake.

   ____

8. This is not my milk.

   ____

9. This is not my orange juice.

   ____

10. These are not my potato chips.

    ____

11. These are not my carrots.

    ____

12. This is not my bag.

    ____

B.3

Put **'** *or* **'s** *where necessary.*

Examples: **A:** Is this Steve report? *(Steve's report)*

B: I don't think so.

A: What are your daughters names? *(daughters' names)*

B: Norma and Carol.

1. **A:** What's Ms. Winston first name?

   B: It's Elenore.

2. **A:** Where's the men room?

   B: It's over there.

3. **A:** Is that your husband brother?

   B: No, that's my brother.

4. **A:** Where are the babies mothers?

   B: In the other room.

5. **A:** Is your school for girls and boys?

   B: No, it's a girls school.

6. **A:** Are your brothers wives friendly?

   B: One is.

7. **A:** Is that your son car?

   B: No, it isn't.

8. **A:** Where's the doctor office?

   B: It's on Cambridge Avenue.

9. **A:** A teacher job is difficult.

   B: I know.

10. **A:** I can't find my teacher.

    B: Look in the teachers room. Many teachers are in there.

B.4

Complete the sentences.

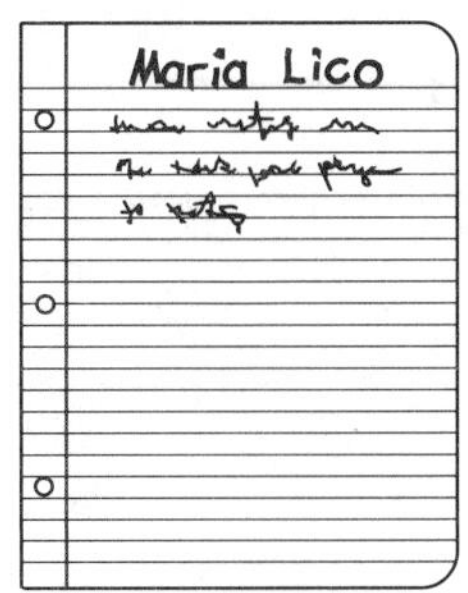

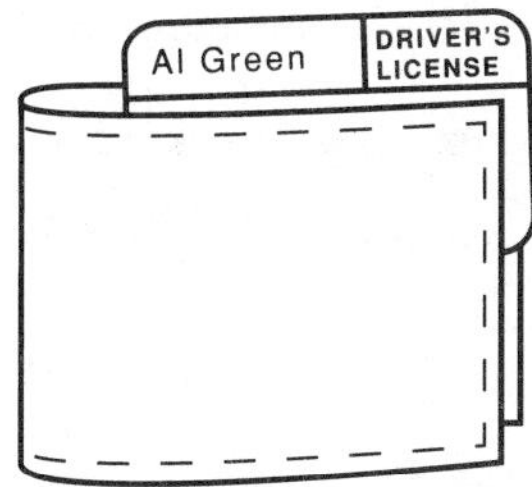

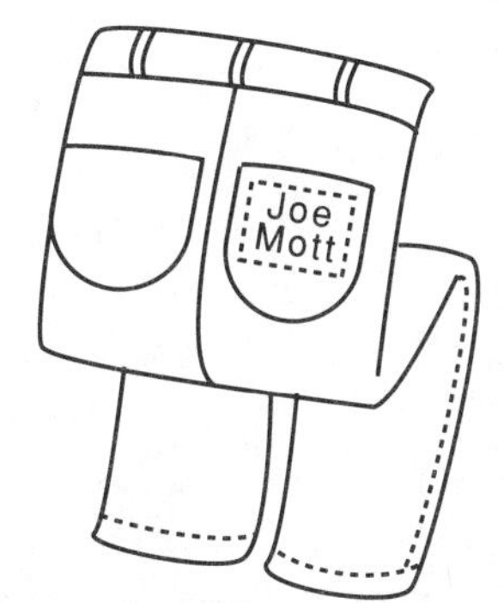

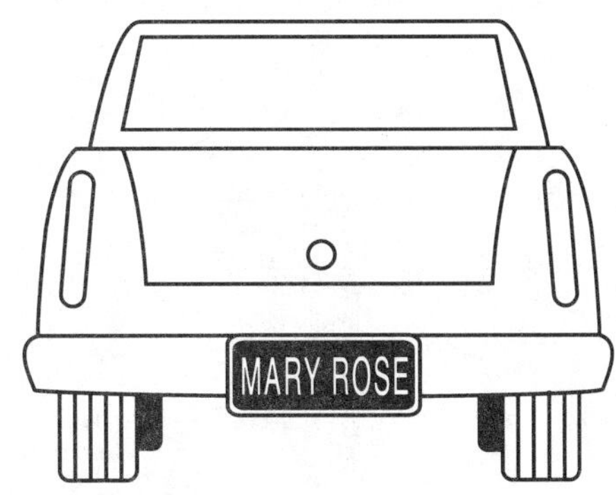

1. The wallet is *Al Green's*.
2. The handbag is ____________________.
3. The car is ____________________.
4. The sweatshirt is ____________________.
5. The notebook is ____________________.
6. The jeans are ____________________.
7. The desk is ____________________.
8. The composition is ____________________.
9. The shoes are ____________________.

C QUESTIONS WITH *WHEN* AND *WHAT*; PREPOSITIONS OF TIME

C.1

Write the words in the correct columns.

4:00
Wednesday
December
June 30th
the morning
night
half past six
the summer
the evening
December 3rd
September 15, 1993
Thursday
1888
May
the spring

AT	IN	ON
4:00	*December*	*Wednesday*

C.2

Michael doesn't have his datebook. It's at your house. He telephones you on September 24. Look at his datebook and answer his questions. Use **at, in,** *or* **on.**

Wed. Sept. 24	Thurs. Sept. 25	Fri. Sept. 26	Sat. Sept. 27
2:30 meeting with director	9 A.M. doctor's appt.	8:30 — piano lesson	Scott's birthday
	3 P.M. job interview	lunch with Nancy Morrison	P.M. Tennis with Henry (after lunch)
	8 P.M. concert	Eve. baseball game	

1. When is my piano lesson on Friday morning?

   It's at 8:30.

2. What time this afternoon is my appointment with the director?

   ______

3. And when is my doctor's appointment tomorrow?

____

4. When's my lunch with Nancy Morrison?

____

5. I know Scott's birthday is this week, but when is it?

____

6. What time is the concert tomorrow?

____

7. I know I have a tennis game with Henry on Saturday. Is it in the morning?

____

8. What about my job interview tomorrow? When's that?

____

9. Is the baseball game on Friday in the afternoon?

____

C.3

Laura is always confused. Write questions.

1. **A:** Is lunch at two o'clock?

   B: No, it isn't.

   A: Then *what time is lunch?*

   B: It's at twelve o'clock.

2. **A:** Is today Monday?

   B: No, it isn't.

   A: Then _______________

   B: It's Sunday.

(Continued on next page.)

3. **A:** Is today June 10th?

   B: No, it isn't.

   A: Then ______________________________

   B: It's June 11th.

4. **A:** Is it 10:30?

   B: No, it isn't.

   A: Then ______________________________

   B: It's 11:30.

5. **A:** Is the meeting today?

   B: No, it isn't.

   A: Then ______________________________

   B: It's tomorrow.

6. **A:** Is the meeting in the afternoon?

   B: No, it isn't.

   A: Then ______________________________

   B: It's in the evening.

7. **A:** The meeting's at six o'clock, isn't it?

   B: No, it isn't.

   A: Then ______________________________

   B: It's at 7:30.

8. **A:** I need some money. Is the bank open on Saturday?

   B: No, it isn't.

   A: Then ______________________________

   B: It's open Monday, Tuesday, Wednesday, Thursday, and Friday.

9. **A:** Is today your birthday?

   B: No, it isn't.

   A: Then ______________________________

   B: It's tomorrow.

D ORDINAL NUMBERS

D.1

Write the numbers.

1. sixth ______6th______
2. forty-fourth ______44th______
3. ninth ____________
4. twelfth ____________
5. twenty-third ____________
6. fifty-first ____________
7. seventy-second ____________
8. eightieth ____________
9. ninety-fifth ____________
10. a hundred and first ____________
11. a hundred and sixteenth ____________
12. two hundredth ____________

D.2

Write the words for the numbers.

1. 4th ______fourth______
2. 38th ______thirty-eighth______
3. 3rd ____________
4. 11th ____________
5. 15th ____________
6. 20th ____________
7. 31st ____________
8. 47th ____________
9. 66th ____________
10. 82nd ____________
11. 99th ____________
12. 103rd ____________

(Continued on next page.)

D.3

Write the street names.

Example:

Third Avenue and Thirty-Second Street

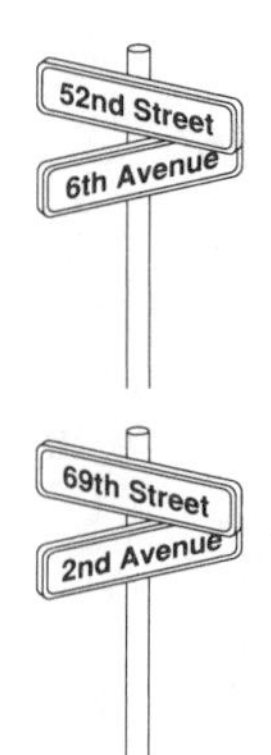

1. ______________________________
2. ______________________________
3. ______________________________
4. ______________________________
5. ______________________________
6. ______________________________

D.4

When are the birthdays of Carol's friends and relatives? Write the dates.

JANUARY						
S	M	T	W	T	F	S
				1 DAN	2	3 ELLEN
4	5	6	7	8	9	10 AUNT VALERIE
11	12	13	14	15	16	17
18	19	20 YOKO	21	22	23	24
25	26	27	28	29	30	31 NORMA

FEBRUARY						
S	M	T	W	T	F	S
1	2 MOM	3	4	5 UNCLE BOB	6	7
8	9 GRANDMA	10	11	12	13	14
15	16	17	18 DOUG	19	20	21 DAD
22 BERTHA	23	24	25	26	27	28

1. When is her father's birthday? *It's on February twenty-first.*
2. When is her mother's birthday? ______________________
3. When is Norma's birthday? ______________________
4. When is Aunt Valerie's birthday? ______________________
5. When is Uncle Bob's birthday? ______________________
6. When is Yoko's birthday? ______________________
7. When is her grandmother's birthday? ______________________
8. When is Ellen's birthday? ______________________
9. When is Doug's birthday? ______________________
10. When is Dan's birthday? ______________________
11. When is Bertha's birthday? ______________________

UNIT

4

Imperatives; There is/There are

A IMPERATIVES; SUGGESTIONS WITH LET'S

A.1

Match the people with their statements.

1. __d__ The teacher said	a. Leave me alone.
2. ______ Mr. Michaels said to his children	b. Open your mouth and say, "Ah."
3. ______ The doctor said	c. Put your hands up.
4. ______ The police officer said	d. Open your books to page 34.
5. ______ Jenny said to her brother	e. Go to bed.

Now do the same with these sentences.

6. ______ The teacher said	f. Don't move.
7. ______ Mr. Michaels said to his children	g. Don't eat so fast.
8. ______ The doctor said	h. Don't bother me.
9. ______ The police officer said	i. Don't talk during the test.
10. ______ Jenny said to her brother	j. Don't take this medicine at night.

A.2

Complete the sentences. Use the verbs in the box.

ask	be	buy	clean	give
go	open	study	talk	tell
use				

1. I'm hot. Please ____open____ the window.
2. That animal is dangerous. ____Don't go____ near it.
3. ________________ your room right now. It's a mess.
4. The baby is asleep. ________________.
5. The apples are bad. ________________ them.
6. We're lost. ________________ the policeofficer for directions.

7. It's a surprise party. __________________ late.

8. This is a secret. __________________ anyone.

9. The test is on Monday. __________________ pages 50 and 51.

10. I'm cold. __________________ me my sweater, please.

11. This glass isn't yours. __________________ it.

A.3

Look at the map and complete the note. Use the verbs in the box.

get off	go	make	ring	take	turn	walk

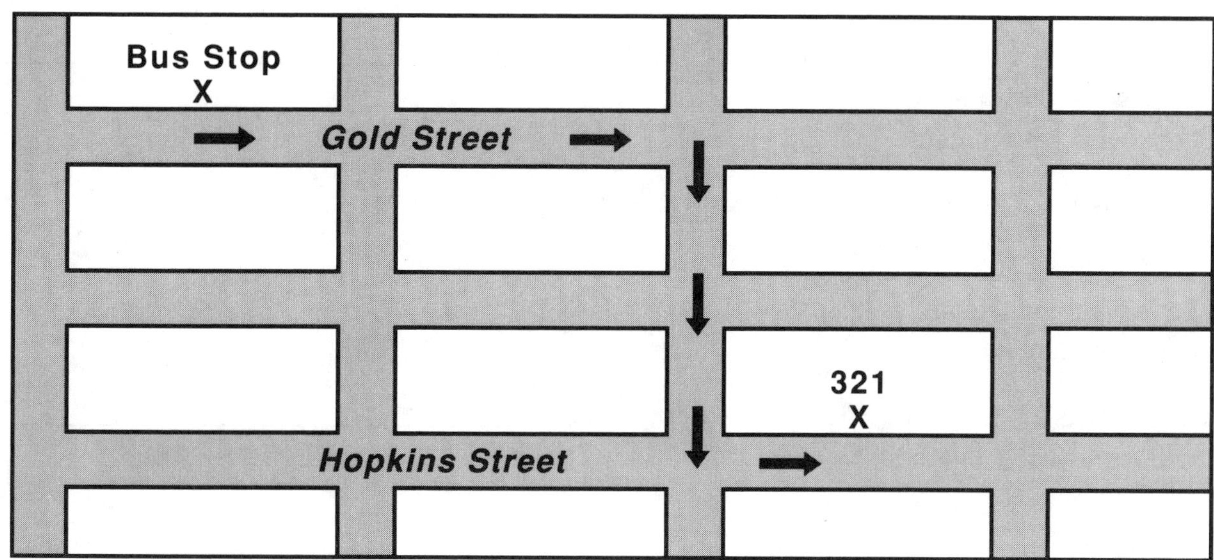

DIRECTIONS

Take (1.) bus twenty-six. __________________ (2.) the bus on Gold Street. __________________ (3.) down Gold Street. At the traffic light, __________________ (4.) right. __________________ (5.) another two blocks. Then __________________ (6.) a left turn. That's Hopkins Street. __________________ (7.) the bell at 321 Hopkins. That's my house.

A.4

Complete the sentences.

1. Students in an English class say to the teacher, "Let's take a break."
   a. Let's take a break.
   b. Let's take a test.

2. Donny says to his brother, "____________________"
   a. Let's clean our room.
   b. Let's play basketball.

3. It's Saturday night, and Pete and Elenore are tired. Elenore says,
   "____________________"
   a. Let's go dancing tonight.
   b. Let's not do anything tonight.

4. It's five o'clock. One secretary says to another secretary, "____________________"
   a. Let's go out for dinner.
   b. Let's work late tonight.

5. Two tourists are in a foreign country. One tourist says to the other,
   "____________________"
   a. Let's visit a museum.
   b. Let's sleep all day.

6. Louisa thinks TV is boring. She says to her boyfriend, "____________________"
   a. Let's not watch TV tonight.
   b. Let's watch TV tonight.

7. It's a beautiful day. Miriam says to her roommate, "____________________"
   a. Let's not forget our umbrellas.
   b. Let's not take the car to class today. Let's walk.

8. It's Pete Winston's birthday. Carol says to Norma, "____________________"
   a. Let's get a present for Dad.
   b. Let's forget about his birthday.

9. Celia and her sister are late. Celia says, "____________________"
   a. Let's take a taxi.
   b. Let's walk.

10. It's cold. Jenny says to her boyfriend, "____________________"
    a. Let's wait outside.
    b. Let's not wait outside.

A.5

Write sentences with **let's**. *Use the expressions in the box.*

get something to eat	go swimming	leave
go inside	go to bed	not invite her to the party
go out and look for him		

1. **A:** I'm tired.

   B: I am, too.

   A: *Let's go to bed.*

2. **A:** I'm hungry.

   B: I am, too.

   A: ______________________________

3. **A:** I'm hot.

   B: I am, too.

   A: ______________________________

4. **A:** I'm cold.

   B: I am, too.

   A: ______________________________

5. **A:** I'm worried about Rocky. Where is he?

   B: I don't know.

   A: ______________________________

6. **A:** I'm angry with Lulu.

   B: I am, too.

   A: ______________________________

7. **A:** I'm bored at this party.

   B: I am, too.

   A: ______________________________

B SUBJECT AND OBJECT PRONOUNS

B.1

Underline the object in each sentence.

1. Please help Yoko and Carol.
2. Peter loves his daughter.
3. Read page 104.
4. Don't ask the teacher.
5. Don't eat my ice cream.
6. Buy five stamps.

B.2

Underline the object pronoun in each sentence.

1. Don't tell him.
2. We love you very much.
3. My mother loves me very much.
4. Put it in our car.
5. Meet her later.
6. The baby is next to us.
7. It is between them.
8. She is near him.

B.3

Complete the chart.

	SUBJECT PRONOUNS	POSSESSIVE ADJECTIVES	OBJECT PRONOUNS
	(**I** am here.)	(This is **my** book.)	(Help **me**.)
1.	I	my	
2.		your	you
3.	he		him
4.		her	
5.	it		
6.		our	
7.	they		

B.4

Complete the sentences. Use **me, you, him, her, our,** *or* **them.**

1. **A:** Is this for Lulu and Bertha?
   B: Yes, it's for *them*.
2. **A:** Is this for me?
   B: Yes, it's for ______________.
3. **A:** Is this for Milt?
   B: Yes, it's for ______________.
4. **A:** Is this for my sister?
   B: Yes, it's for ______________.
5. **A:** Is this for you?
   B: Yes, it's for ______________.
6. **A:** Is this for her father?
   B: Yes, it's for ______________.
7. **A:** Is this for you and me?
   B: Yes, it's for ______________.
8. **A:** Is this for the dogs?
   B: Yes, it's for ______________.
9. **A:** Is this for the children?
   B: Yes, it's for ______________.
10. **A:** Is this for your grandmother?
    B: Yes, it's for ______________.
11. **A:** Is this for Yoko?
    B: Yes, it's for ______________.
12. **A:** Is this for my classmates and me?
    B: Yes, it's for ______________.

B.5

Write sentences.

1. love/you/I

   I love you.

2. him/she/loves

   ____

3. us/love/they

   ____

4. we/them/love

   ____

5. the answer/tell/me

   ____

6. show/her/the paper

   ____

7. them/take/some flowers

   ____

8. me/a postcard/send

   ____

B.6

Complete the sentences. Use a subject pronoun or an object pronoun.

1. **A:** Is your name Doug?

   B: Yes, ____*it*____ is.

2. **A:** This record is for you. ______________'s for your birthday.

   B: Oh, thank you. I love ______________.

3. **A:** Is Bertha your aunt?

   B: Yes, ______________ is.

   A: Please give ______________ this package.

4. **A:** My brother is over there.

   B: I like ______________. ______________ is handsome.

5. **A:** Are you busy?

   B: Yes, ______________ am. Please call ______________ later.

6. **A:** Here are two dishes.

   B: But ______________'re dirty. Please wash ______________.

7. **A:** Are you and Lee free on Sunday?

   B: Yes, ______________ are. Visit ______________ then.

8. **A:** Hello?

   B: Hello. Is Judi there?

   A: Yes. Just a minute. Judi! Judi! The phone's for ______________.

C THERE IS/THERE ARE

C.1

Complete the conversation. Use **there is** *or* **there are**.

A: Is anyone in the house?

B: Yes, ___there are___ (1.) two men. ______________ (2.) also a woman. Oh, ______________ (3.) two little boys, too.

A: And in the yard?

B: ______________ (4.) a dog, and ______________ (5.) three other children.

A: What's in the garage?

B: ______________ (6.) some boxes.

A: What's in them?

B: I don't know, but ______________ (7.) also a motorcycle. ______________ (8.) two cars, too.

A: Two?

B: Uh-huh. ______________ (9.) a TV there, too.

A: A TV? In the garage? That's strange.

B: And ______________ (10.) a sofa.

A: That's really strange!

C.2

Write sentences.

1. clothes/the closet/are/in/there

   There are clothes in the closet.

2. is/the table/a/there/on/knife

   ____

(Continued on next page.)

3. the garage/there/cars/in/are/two

___

4. flowers/there/the garden/in/are

___

5. dog/the bed/is/under/a/there

___

6. between/there/the two chairs/a/is/box

___

7. is/there/the wall/a/on/picture

___

8. are/five/there/the floor/books/on

___

9. seven/in/there/this/house/rooms/are

___

C.3

What's unusual about the tree? Write sentences. Use **there is** *or* **there are**.

1. *There is a telephone in the tree.*
2. *There are suitcases in the tree.*

3. ______________________________

4. ______________________________

5. ______________________________

6. ______________________________

7. ______________________________

8. ______________________________

9. ______________________________

10. ______________________________

11. ______________________________

12. ______________________________

13. ______________________________

C.4

Write sentences about Vacation Hotel. Use **there is, there isn't, there are,** *or* **there aren't.**

VACATION HOTEL

In every room:
- a bathroom
- two beds
- two closets
- a television
- an air conditioner

At the hotel:
- two restaurants
- four tennis courts
- two parking lots

1. (a bathroom in every room) *There is a bathroom in every room.*
2. (a radio in every room) *There isn't a radio in every room.*
3. (two beds in every room) ______________________________
4. (two closets in every room) ______________________________
5. (a telephone in every room) ______________________________
6. (a television in every room) ______________________________
7. (an air conditioner in every room) ______________________________

(Continued on next page.)

8. (a refrigerator in every room) __________
9. (a swimming pool at the hotel) __________
10. (restaurants at the hotel) __________
11. (tennis courts at the hotel) __________
12. (tourist shops at the hotel) __________
13. (parking lots at the hotel) __________

C.5

Write sentences. Use **there are, there aren't, they are,** *or* **they aren't.**

What's in *Lawrenceville?*

Bakeries	**2**	*Not open on Sundays*
Department stores	**0**	
Banks	**2**	*On Main Street*
Clothing stores	**3**	*Not very expensive*
Bookstores	**0**	
Drugstores	**4**	*Small*
Gas stations	**3**	*In the center of town*
Hospitals	**0**	
Movie theaters	**0**	
Restaurants	**2**	*Open for lunch and dinner*
Schools	**3**	*Not far from Main Street*
Supermarkets	**2**	*Big*
Swimming pools	**0**	

1. *There are two bakeries. They aren't open on Sundays.*
2. *There aren't any department stores.*
3. __________
4. __________
5. __________
6. __________
7. __________
8. __________

9. ______________________________

10. ______________________________

11. ______________________________

12. ______________________________

13. ______________________________

D NUMBERS AND QUANTIFIERS

D.1

Put a check (✓) next to the correct sentence for each number.

1. Thirty eggs
   a. There are a few eggs in the refrigerator. _____
   b. There are a lot of eggs in the refrigerator. __✓__

2. Three books
   a. There are several books on the desk. _____
   b. There are many books on the desk. _____

3. Zero people
   a. There are not any people in the room. _____
   b. There are not many people in the room. _____

4. Two apples
   a. There are not any apples in the bag. _____
   b. There are not many apples in the bag. _____

5. Ten people
   a. There are several people in the car. _____
   b. There are many people in the car. _____

6. Four cars
   a. There are some cars in the parking lot. _____
   b. There are a lot of cars in the parking lot. _____

7. Zero washing machines
   a. There are not any washing machines in the apartment. _____
   b. There are not many washing machines in the apartment. _____

(Continued on next page.)

8. Fifty shirts
   a. There are a few shirts in the closet. _____
   b. There are a lot of shirts in the closet. _____

9. Five boxes
   a. There are several boxes on the table. _____
   b. There are many boxes on the table. _____

D.2

Complete the sentences. Use words from each column.

CLASS ROSTER			
Agustin Aldovar	Venezuela	Muhammad Nur	Egypt
Mehmet Beyoglu	Turkey	Chie Oshima	Japan
Chou-Hsin Chen	China		
Teresa Gomez	Mexico	Christina Paschow	Greece
Pablo Gonzalez	Venezuela	Jaime Rodriguez	Venezuela
Jeonghyun Hong	Korea	Jose Sanchez	Venezuela
Su Yuan Huang	China		
Tomohiro Iwasaki	Japan	Alejandro Santiago	Mexico
Min Jung	Korea	Laura Sepulveda	Venezuela
Yuko Koyama	Japan	Sylvia Suarez	Venezuela
Yong Lee	Korea	Miyako Tamaki	Japan
Maria Martinez	Mexico	Karina Torrijos	Venezuela
Takashi Miki	Japan	Yang Ling Tsu	China
Mariko Morimoto	Japan	Keiko Tsukamoto	Japan
Margarita Munoz	Mexico	So Young	Korea

is are aren't	a any a few many	student students

1. There ___*is*___ ___*a*___ ___*student*___ from Egypt.
2. There ___*are*___ ___*a few*___ ___*students*___ from Korea.
3. There __________ __________ ______________ from Russia.
4. There __________ __________ ______________ from Japan.
5. There __________ __________ ______________ from Venezuela.
6. There __________ __________ ______________ from Turkey.

7. There ______________ ______________ __________________ from Morocco.

8. There ______________ ______________ __________________ from Greece.

9. There ______________ ______________ __________________ from Mexico.

10. There ______________ ______________ __________________ from Indonesia.

11. There ______________ ______________ __________________ from China.

12. There ______________ ______________ __________________ from France.

E QUESTIONS WITH *IS THERE, ARE THERE,* AND *HOW MANY*

E.1

Look at the picture and answer the questions. Use short answers.

1. Are there any apples? *Yes, there are.*

2. Are there any pears? ______________________________

3. Are there any grapes? ______________________________

(Continued on next page.)

4. Are there any cherries? ____________________
5. Are there any oranges? ____________________
6. Are there any peaches? ____________________
7. Are there any pineapples? ____________________
8. Are there any watermelons? ____________________
9. Are there any grapefruits? ____________________

E.2

Write questions. Then answer them.

1. many elephants in Florida
   Are there many elephants in Florida? — No, there aren't.
2. many elephants in India
   ____________________ ____________________
3. a desert in Canada
   ____________________ ____________________
4. camels in Saudi Arabia
   ____________________ ____________________
5. a long river in the Sahara Desert
   ____________________ ____________________
6. many lions in Russia
   ____________________ ____________________
7. mountains in Kenya
   ____________________ ____________________
8. people in the Antarctic
   ____________________ ____________________
9. big city in Thailand
   ____________________ ____________________
10. a monkey in your garden
    ____________________ ____________________

E.3

Look at the picture in exercise C.3 on page 48. Write questions. Use **how many**.

1. *How many televisions are there?* ______ There are two.
2. ______ There is one.
3. ______ There are three.
4. ______ There are four.
5. ______ There are five.
6. ______ There are six.
7. ______ There are seven.
8. ______ There are eight.
9. ______ There are nine.
10. ______ There are ten.

F AND/BUT

F.1

Add commas where necessary.

Examples:	The house is small and expensive.	(No comma)
	The car is small, and it is in the parking lot.	(Add a comma)

1. There are beautiful flowers and a box of chocolates on the table.
2. It is for you but it is not for your birthday.
3. There is another box under the table and it is big.
4. It is for you and your husband.
5. The shirt is for your husband and the jacket is for you.
6. The jacket is warm but it is not for the winter.
7. The jacket is beautiful and it is just my style.
8. This is very kind of you but not necessary.

F.2

Complete the sentences.

1. Alice is a good basketball player and ___a good tennis player___.
   a. a bad tennis player
   b. a good tennis player
2. The house is big, but ______________________. It's not for us.
   a. it's beautiful
   b. it's far from the center of town
3. The book is very long, but ______________________.
   a. it's interesting
   b. it's boring
4. Bill is a good worker, and ______________________.
   a. his wife is not
   b. his wife is, too
5. There's a big bag in the other room, but ______________________.
   a. it's not my bag
   b. it's a small bag
6. Open the door, but ______________________.
   a. go out
   b. don't go out
7. He is a little fat but ______________________.
   a. healthy
   b. unhealthy
8. The dog is not friendly, and ______________________.
   a. I'm afraid
   b. it's a good dog

F.3

Complete the sentences with the phrases below. Don't forget to use commas.

a. but it's always crowded
b. but there are only a few people in the restaurant
c. and I'm sick
d. but I'm not in it
e. but they're not very good
f. and we're very proud
g. and there's no hot water
h. but they're comfortable
i. and there are always a lot of people
j. and we're very unhappy

1. I'm tired, *and I'm sick* ______
2. This is a picture of my family ______
3. There are many cars in the parking lot ______
4. There's no air conditioner ______
5. These shoes are not very pretty ______
6. These hamburgers are big ______
7. The restaurant isn't very good ______
8. The museum's on Fifth Avenue ______
9. Our dog's lost ______
10. Our daughter's a great artist ______

UNIT

5

Present Progressive

A PRESENT PROGRESSIVE: AFFIRMATIVE AND NEGATIVE STATEMENTS

A.1

Match the statement with the sentence.

1. d Lou's at the supermarket.
2. ______ Paul's at the bank.
3. ______ Linda's in the library.
4. ______ The football players are on the field.
5. ______ The doctor's at the hospital.
6. ______ Doug's at the shopping mall.
7. ______ Susan's in the bathroom.
8. ______ Mrs. Thompson and her family ______ are in the dining room.
9. ______ Sharon and her boyfriend are ______ at the beach.
10. ______ Mark's at the office.

a. They're playing football.
b. She's studying.
c. She's examining a patient.
d. He's buying groceries.
e. He's getting some money.
f. They're having dinner.
g. She's taking a shower.
h. They're lying in the sun.
i. He's writing a report.
j. He's buying a shirt.

A.2

Write the base form or the present participle of the verb.

BASE FORM	PRESENT PARTICIPLE	BASE FORM	PRESENT PARTICIPLE
1. have	having	9. ______	running
2. sit	sitting	10. hit	______
3. get	______	11. ______	talking
4. shine	______	12. drive	______
5. ______	raining	13. do	______
6. ______	making	14. ______	putting
7. watch	______	15. ______	beginning
8. listen	______	16. study	______

A.3

Write true sentences.

1. I/do/a grammar exercise

   I am doing a grammar exercise.

2. I/sleep

   I am not sleeping.

3. I/have/a good time

   ____

4. The sun/shine

   ____

5. It/rain

   ____

6. It/get/dark

   ____

7. I/listen/to the radio

   ____

8. I/ talk/on the phone

   ____

9. I/sit/on a chair

   ____

10. My best friend/sit/next to me

    ____

11. My neighbors/make/a lot of noise

    ____

12. I/write/with a pencil

    ____

A.4

Complete the postcard. Use the correct form of the verbs in parentheses.

January 11

Greetings from Vermont from all of us. We (have) ___are having___ a great time. It
1.
(snow) ________________ a little right now, and it is cold. Many people (ski) ________________, but we
2. 3.
are too tired. We (relax) ________________, at the moment. Ellen and I (sit) ________________ in the cof-
4. 5.
fee shop. She (read) ________________ and I (write) ________________ to you! The girls (make)
6. 7.
________________ a snowman outside. They (enjoy) ________________ themselves a lot. Tommy (play)
8. 9.
________________ a video game—naturally!
10.
We hope you are well.

Love from all of us,

Nick

B PRESENT PROGRESSIVE: *YES/NO* QUESTIONS AND SHORT ANSWERS

B.1

Write questions.

1. doing/you/a grammar exercise/are

   ___Are you doing a grammar exercise?___

2. glasses/wearing/you/are

   ____

3. your English teacher/correcting/is/papers

   ____

4. TV/you and a friend/watching/are

____

5. your classmates/doing/this exercise/now/are

____

6. are/having/your neighbors/dinner

____

7. shining/the sun/is

____

8. your friends/are/for you/waiting

____

9. working/are/your parents

____

10. ice cream/eating/are/you

____

11. is/helping/your teacher/you/with this exercise

____

12. outside/children/are/playing

____

B.2

Answer the questions in exercise B1. Use short answers. If you don't know an answer, write **I don't know.**

1. (Are you doing a grammar exercise?)

   Yes, I am.

2. ____________________
3. ____________________
4. ____________________
5. ____________________
6. ____________________
7. ____________________
8. ____________________
9. ____________________
10. ____________________
11. ____________________
12. ____________________

B.3

Write questions. Use the verbs and expressions in parentheses.

1. **A:** Yoko's in class
   B: *Is she listening to the teacher?* (listen to the teacher)
   A: Probably.
2. A: Mary's in the bedroom. (sleep)
   B: ____________________
   A: Maybe
3. **A:** All the children are at the playground. (play)
   B: ____________________
   A: Probably.
4. **A:** My son and his friend are at the swimming pool. (swim)
   B: ____________________
   A: I think so.
5. **A:** John's in the post office. (buy stamps)
   B: ____________________
   A: Probably.
6. **A:** My parents are on vacation. (have a good time)
   B: ____________________
   A: I hope so.
7. **A:** Carol's at the hospital. (visit someone)
   B: ____________________
   A: I don't know.
8. **A:** Warren and Anne are outside. (play tennis)
   B: ____________________
   A: I think so.

9. **A:** Julie's under the car. (fix something)

   B: ______________________________

   A: Maybe.

10. **A:** Michael isn't here yet. (come)

    B: ______________________________

    A: I think so.

11. **A:** There are two people in the hall. (wait for me)

    B: ______________________________

    A: I don't know.

12. **A:** A man's behind you. (follow me)

    B: ______________________________

    A: I don't know.

C PRESENT PROGRESSIVE: *WH-* QUESTIONS

C.1

Look at the picture and answer the questions.

1. What is Doug buying? *A pineapple.*
2. What is the storekeeper weighing? ______________________________

(Continued on next page.)

3. Why are the people standing in line? ______________________

4. Who is wearing a black coat? ______________________

5. Where are the people standing? ______________________

6. What is the young woman wearing? ______________________

7. Where is the young woman standing? ______________________

C.2

Write questions.

1. leaving/are/why/you/so early

   Why are you leaving so early?

2. the gift/where/you/are/hiding

   ____

3. is/on the door/who/knocking

   ____

4. your/are/what/children/wearing

   ____

5. waiting for/she/who/is

   ____

6. you/looking for/what/are

   ____

7. they/are/why/to work/walking

   ____

8. are/the baby/where/they/taking

   ____

9. is/sending/him/why/a gift/she

____

10. doing/you/what/are

____

C.3

Write the correct questions from exercise C.2.

1. ____Why are they walking to work?____

   Their car isn't working.

2. ____

   I'm fixing the lamp.

3. ____

   I'm bored.

4. ____

   My keys.

5. ____

   Under the bed.

6. ____

   I think it's the mailman.

7. ____

   T-shirts and blue jeans.

8. ____

   Her boyfriend.

9. ____

   It's his birthday.

10. ____

    To the doctor.

C.4

Complete the questions.

1. **A:** What are you doing?

   B: I'm talking on the phone.

   A: Who ___are you talking___ to?
   a. is talking
   b. are you talking

   B: A friend.

2. **A:** What are you doing?

   B: I'm cooking for the party.

   A: Who ________________ to the party?
   a. is coming
   b. are they coming

   B: Some people from work.

3. **A:** Where's Kevin?

   B: He's playing in the backyard.

   A: Who ________________ with?
   a. is playing
   b. is he playing

   B: Some friends from school.

4. **A:** The music is nice.

   B: Yes, it is.

   A: Who ________________ ?
   a. is playing
   b. is he playing

   B: My son.

5. **A:** What are you doing?

   B: I'm writing a letter.

   A: Who ________________ ?
   a. is writing
   b. are you writing to

   B: My cousin.

6. **A:** Are the kids at home?

   B: No, they're helping someone with some packages.

   A: Who ______________________ ?
   a. is helping
   b. are they helping

   B: The elderly couple down the street.

7. **A:** Nurse Richards, is anybody still waiting in the office?

   B: Yes.

   A: Who ______________________ ?
   a. is waiting
   b. are they waiting

   B: Ms. Gomez and Mr. Robertson.

C.5

Write questions.

1. **A:** Doug is painting something.

   B: *What is he painting?*

   A: I'm not sure. I think it's a portrait.

2. **A:** I'm reading.

   B: ______________________________

   A: The newspaper.

3. **A:** The kids are eating.

   B: ______________________________

   A: Some ice cream.

4. **A:** My husband's cooking.

   B: ______________________________

   A: Dinner.

5. **A:** Someone's coming.

   B: ______________________________

   A: I think it's your sister.

6. **A:** I'm going to bed.

(Continued on next page.)

B: ______________________________

A: I'm tired.

7. **A:** We're going.

   B: ______________________________

   A: To the supermarket.

8. **A:** I'm selling my car.

   B: ______________________________

   A: It's old.

9. **A:** Monica and Chris are swimming.

   B: ______________________________

   A: At the pool near the park.

10. **A:** I'm watching TV.

    B: ______________________________

    A: A baseball game.

11. **A:** The police officers are watching someone.

    B: ______________________________

    A: That young man over there.

12. **A:** Carol's dating someone new.

    B: ______________________________

    A: Eric Snyder.

D PRESENT PROGRESSIVE: EXTENDED TIME

D.1

Write **right now** *or* **these days** *about each sentence.*

1. Prices are getting higher. *these days*
2. Are you coming? *right now*

3. I'm getting you some water. ______________________
4. We're getting in the car. ______________________
5. The baby's getting bigger. ______________________
6. Why are you crying? ______________________
7. Why is she doing badly at school? ______________________
8. Where are you going to school? ______________________
9. My girlfriend and I are not enjoying ourselves. ______________________
10. The students are not learning much. ______________________

D.2

Complete the newspaper article. Use the correct form of the verbs in parentheses.

NO END TO RISE IN PRICES

(you/spend) *Are you spending* (1.) more on bread and cheese these days? Yes, you (probably say) ______ (2.). In fact, you (probably spend) ______ (3.) more on almost all of your food. Everything (go) ______ (4.) up, and many people (not make) ______ (5.) more money. That's why life (get) ______ (6.) so difficult for many working people.

What (the government/do) ______ (7.) about it? (it/do) ______ (8.) anything? "No," says Martha Norton. "We (look) ______ (9.) for help, but the government (not give) ______ (10.) us any." Many people are unhappy and (complain) ______ (11.). They (write) ______ (12.) to the president and other people in the government. Who (you/write) ______ (13.) to?

UNIT 6

Simple Present Tense

A SIMPLE PRESENT TENSE: AFFIRMATIVE AND NEGATIVE STATEMENTS

A.1

Read the job descriptions and answer the questions. Use the words in the box.

cook	flight attendant	pilot	salesperson
doctor	mechanic	professor	secretary

1. Daniel fixes cars. He works in a garage. What is he?

   He's a mechanic.

2. Dina and Lesley answer telephones and type letters. They work in a college office. What are they?

3. Captain Phillips goes to the airport every day. He flies airplanes. What is he?

4. Kay Williams gives lectures and meets with students. She works in a university. What is she?

5. Ben and Rachel work on an airplane. They serve meals and drinks to passengers. What are they?

6. I work in a restaurant. I prepare the food. What am I?

7. I work in a store. I sell refrigerators. What am I?

8. Ellen helps sick people. She works in a hospital. What is she?

A.2

Complete each sentence with the correct verb. Use the simple present tense.

1. Mary is a taxi driver. She ___drives___ a taxi.
2. Stuart is a Spanish teacher. He ____________ Spanish.
3. Maria Domingo is a singer. She ____________.
4. Nassos Morona is a dancer. He ____________.
5. Bill Bright is a baseball player. He ____________ baseball.
6. Shirley Simpson is a bank manager. She ____________ a bank.
7. Sam and Victor are trash collectors. They ____________ trash.
8. Margaret and Phil are house painters. They ____________ houses.
9. Lou is a window washer. He ____________ windows.
10. Oscar, Tom, and Steve are firefighters. They ____________ fires.

A.3

Complete the sentences. Use **don't** *or* **doesn't.**

1. Doug lives in New York, but Carol ___doesn't___.
2. Carol lives in Oregon, but her parents ___don't___.
3. Carol has a roommate, but Doug ____________.
4. Doug has green eyes, but Norma ____________.
5. Elenore and Pete live in New York, but Bertha and Lulu ____________.
6. Doug's friend, Norman, has a brother, but Doug ____________.
7. Yoko studies hard, but Carol and Doug ____________.
8. Carol likes her way of life at college, but Pete and Elenore ____________.
9. Some students think English grammar is easy, but I ____________.
10. My teacher likes this grammar exercise, but my classmates and I ____________.

A.4

Complete the conversation. Use the correct form of the verbs in parentheses.

A: Tell me about you and your family.

B: My husband and I (be) ___are___ (1.) pretty traditional. I (take) ________ (2.) care of the home, and he (go) ________ (3.) to work. He (have) ________ (4.) a business in town, but we (live) ________ (5.) in an old house in the country.

A: Alone?

B: Oh, no. We (not live) ________ (6.) alone. We (have) ________ (7.) eight children, seven boys and one girl. Two of them (not live) ________ (8.) with us any more. Our daughter (be) ________ (9.) married, and she (live) ________ (10.) with her family. She (have) ________ (11.) two children. One of our sons (be) ________ (12.) also married, but he (not have) ________ (13.) any children. Our other six sons (live) ________ (14.) with us. One of them, Marvin, (study) ________ (15.) at the local college and (work) ________ (16.) part-time. He (leave) ________ (17.) home every morning at around six o'clock and (not come) ________ (18.) home until seven or eight in the evening. It (not be) ________ (19.) a good schedule at all. Our son Russell (help) ________ (20.) my husband, and the other boys (go) ________ (21.) to high school.

A: Are you busy all the time?

B: Oh, yes. I (not have) ________ (22.) much free time at all. That's why we (try) ________ (23.) to rest on Sundays. We (not get) ________ (24.) up until nine o'clock.

A.5

Correct the sentences. Choose words from the box.

a big population	grass	the sun
during the day	mice	0° C
in the east	Antarctic	100° C
a hot climate	sand	big ears

1. The Sun rises in the west.

   The Sun doesn't rise in the west. It rises in the east.

2. Water boils at 90° C.

3. Water freezes at 5° C.

4. The Sun goes around the Earth.

5. Penguins come from the Arctic.

6. Cows eat meat.

7. China has a small population.

8. Deserts have a lot of water.

9. Elephants have small ears.

10. Egypt has a cold climate.

(Continued on next page.)

11. The sun shines at night.

____

12. Mice run after cats.

____

B SIMPLE PRESENT TENSE: *YES/NO* QUESTIONS AND SHORT ANSWERS

B.1

Write the questions in the correct boxes.

1. Do you feel a pain here?
2. Do you know how to type?
3. Do you want a plastic bag or a paper bag?
4. Do you have any experience?
5. Do you want a one-bedroom or a two-bedroom apartment?
6. Do you get many headaches?
7. Do you have any other fresh fish?
8. Do you speak a foreign language?
9. Do you want a place near the center of town?
10. Does your back hurt?
11. Does this orange juice cost $2.50?
12. Does the house have two bathrooms?

A. PEOPLE OFTEN ASK THIS AT A JOB INTERVIEW	B. PEOPLE OFTEN ASK THIS AT A DOCTOR'S OFFICE
	Do you feel a pain here?
C. PEOPLE OFTEN ASK THIS AT A REAL ESTATE OFFICE	**D. PEOPLE OFTEN ASK THIS AT A SUPERMARKET**

B.2

Match the questions and answers.

1. __e__ Does the Sun go around the Earth?
2. ______ Do banks have money?
3. ______ Do you speak English perfectly?
4. ______ Does England have many mountains?
5. ______ Do supermarkets sell swimming pools?
6. ______ Does it snow a lot in Sweden?
7. ______ Does the president of the United States live in the White House?
8. ______ Do you eat every day?

a. Yes, it does.
b. No, they don't.
c. No, I don't.
d. Yes, I do.
e. No, it doesn't.
f. Yes, they do.
g. No, it doesn't.
h. Yes, he does.

B.3

Answer the questions. Use short answers.

	MICHAEL	MARY	KAREN	LARRY
ROCK MUSIC	✓	X	X	X
CLASSICAL MUSIC	X	✓	X	✓
JAZZ	X	✓	X	✓
COUNTRY MUSIC	X	✓	X	X
FOLK MUSIC	✓	X	X	✓

✓=YES X=NO

1. Does Michael like rock music? __*Yes, he does.*__
2. Do Karen and Larry like country music? __*No, they don't.*__
3. Does Mary like jazz? ______________________
4. Does Karen like folk music? ______________________
5. Do Michael and Larry like folk music? ______________________
6. Does Larry like jazz? ______________________
7. Does Mary like folk music? ______________________
8. Does Larry like classical music? ______________________

(Continued on next page.)

9. Do Karen and Larry like rock music? ______________________

10. Do Mary and Larry like jazz? ______________________

B.4

Find the mistake in each sentence. Then correct the mistake.

1. ~~You~~ *Do you* need any help?

2. Does your roommate likes your girlfriend?

3. The teacher wear glasses?

4. Do Mr. Flagg have a car?

5. Does Jack and Jill sleep until ten o'clock?

6. Peter eat fast?

7. Are she leave for work at the same time every day?

8. Is the dog eat two times a day?

9. Does the doctor has your telephone number?

10. Football players play in the summer?

B.5

Complete the questions.

1. People do not come here on Sundays.

   Do they come on Saturdays?

2. Carol has class on Mondays and Wednesdays.

   ______________________ class on Tuesdays, too?

3. The children like bananas.

   ______________________ apples, too?

4. We live in a house.

   ______________________ in a big house?

5. My boyfriend knows my brother.

   ______________________ your sister?

6. My wife and I want a hotel room.

    ______________________ a room for one or two nights?

7. I have two sisters.

    ______________________ any brothers?

8. The car does not belong to Mr. Winchester.

    ______________________ to Mrs. Winchester?

9. My classmates and I do not like grammar exercises.

    ______________________ vocabulary exercises?

10. I do not know the answer to the first question.

    ______________________ the answer to the second question?

11. The saleswomen do not work in the afternoon.

    ______________________ in the morning?

12. That young man does not come from the United States.

    ______________________ from Canada?

C SIMPLE PRESENT TENSE: *WH-* QUESTIONS

C.1

Write the correct question words. Use **who, what, where, when, what time,** *or* **why**.

1. ___What___? a. Orange juice and cereal.
2. ___Why___? b. Because I'm tired.
3. __________? c. At City Central Bank.
4. __________? d. A suit and tie.
5. __________? e. My teacher.
6. __________? f. At noon.
7. __________? g. His parents.
8. __________? h. At his school.

(Continued on next page.)

9. ____________? i. In the morning.

10. ____________? j. Because I want to buy a sweatshirt.

11. ____________? k. At 6:00 in the morning.

12. ____________? l. In August.

C.2

Write questions.

1. want/to leave/do/why/you

   Why do you want to leave?

2. for breakfast/what/you/have/do

   ____

3. get up/husband/does/what time/your

   ____

4. your/corrects/homework/who

   ____

5. does/work/Rosita/where

   ____

6. on vacation/when/go/you and your family/do

   ____

7. what/to work/wear/you/do

   ____

8. need/do/more money/you/why

   ____

9. the/what time/eat/kids/do/lunch

   ____

10. come/the/mail/does/when

    ____

11. Doug/his friends/meet/where/does

____

12. visit/does/on Sundays/Milt/who

____

C.3

Match the questions in exercise C.2 with the answers in exercise C.1. Use each item only once.

1. *Why do you want to leave?* ______ *Because I'm tired.*
2. ______________________ ______________
3. ______________________ ______________
4. ______________________ ______________
5. ______________________ ______________
6. ______________________ ______________
7. ______________________ ______________
8. ______________________ ______________
9. ______________________ ______________
10. ______________________ ______________
11. ______________________ ______________
12. ______________________ ______________

C.4

Complete the sentences. Use **who, what, where, when, what time**, *or* **why**.

Rob: Mom, I'm leaving.

Mom: *Why* (1.)?

Rob: I have a date.

Mom: ________ (2.) is your date?

Rob: At 8:00.

Mom: ________ (3.) do you have a date with?

Rob: With Susie.

(Continued on next page.)

Mom: ____________ does Susie live?
4.

Rob: On Franklin Street.

Mom: ____________ does Susie do?
5.

Rob: She's a student like me, and she has a part-time job.

Mom: ____________ does she work?
6.

Rob: On Saturdays and Sundays.

Mom: ____________ does she work?
7.

Rob: At Cerrano's—you know, the supermarket.

Mom: That's far away. ____________ takes her there and picks her up?
8.

Rob: I don't know. Her parents, probably.

Mom: ____________ do you like her?
9.

Rob: She's nice.

Mom: Yes, but ____________ do you know about her?
10.

Rob: I know that she's nice.

C.5

Write the questions. Use **who, what, where, when, what time,** *or* **why.**

1. *What time do you go to bed?*

   I go to bed at around 11:00.

2. ______________________________

   I drive my children to school because their school is far away.

3. ______________________________

   Pilots? They fly planes.

4. ______________________________

   I think the bank opens at 8:30.

5. ______________________________

   I love you.

6. ______________________________

   One of my brothers lives in New York, and the other lives in Philadelphia.

7. ______________________________

My mother usually does the shopping, but sometimes my father does.

8. ______________________________

I'm not sure. I think most American children start school when they're five years old.

9. ______________________________

In the big white house? I think an old man and woman live there.

10. ______________________________

We stay home and relax on the weekend.

11. ______________________________

Not me. Ask Kate about your keys.

12. ______________________________

The doctor wants to see *you* first.

D SIMPLE PRESENT TENSE AND *THIS/THAT/THESE/THOSE*

D.1

Complete the conversation. Use **that** *or* **those**.

A: Are you enjoying the party?

B: Yes, very much. But I don't know a lot of the people. Who's ___*that*___ (1.) handsome guy over there?

A: My cousin, Dennis.

B: And ____________ (2.) two people?

A: Which people?

B: ____________ (3.) people in the corner.

A: They're also my cousins.

B: Don't tell me ____________ (4.) woman on the sofa is also your cousin.

(Continued on next page.)

A: No, ____________'s my Aunt Phyllis.
5.

B: And is ____________ man next to her her husband?
6.

A: No, ____________'s her brother, my Uncle Norman.
7.

B: What about ____________ kids in the bedroom?
8.

A: Some of them are cousins, but ____________ two at the door are my sisters.
9.

B: You have a big family. Are ____________ nice-looking women near the kitchen your relatives, too?
10.

A: No, the one with the blonde hair is my girlfriend, but I don't know the other woman.

D.2

Complete the sentences. Use **this, that, these,** *or* **those.**

1. Robert and his wife are sitting in their new car. Robert says, "I like ____________ car."
2. Doris looks out the window and sees someone. She doesn't know the person. Doris says,"Who's ____________?"
3. A friend has a gift for Ted and puts a small box in his hand. Ted says, "What's ____________?"
4. Sylvia and Elizabeth are at a party. Sylvia says to Elizabeth, "Isn't ____________ a great party?"
5. Vicky and Peggy are looking in the window of a shoe store. Vicky says to Penny, "Aren't ____________ shoes beautiful?"
6. Vicky and Peggy are in the store now. Vicky has the shoes in her hand. Vicky says, "____________ shoes really are beautiful."
7. Mr. Graham comes into his office. He asks his secretary about some people in the waiting room. Mr. Graham says, "Are ____________ people waiting for me?"
8. Richard and Sandy are looking for their car in the parking lot. Richard finally sees it. It's behind four other cars. Richard says, "____________'s our car. Do you see it?"
9. Frank is at the kitchen table. There's a dish of potatoes in front of him. Frank says to his brother, "____________ are my potatoes. Don't eat them."
10. Mr. and Mrs. Moreno are in their car. They're lost. Mr. Moreno sees a sign about fifty meters away. He says to his wife, "What does ____________ sign say?"

E ONE/ONES

E.1

Match the sentences and responses.

1. ___d___ Do you want the big box?
2. ______ I like the black pants.
3. ______ Is this towel for me?
4. ______ I like the sneakers.
5. ______ Please give me that eraser.
6. ______ Which dogs do you like?
7. ______ Are there any movie theaters near here?
8. ______ Do you want these cookies?

a. No, it's dirty. Take this one.
b. Which one?
c. The brown ones.
d. No, give me the small one.
e. No, give me the chocolate ones.
f. Yes, there's one on Broadway.
g. I don't. I like the gray ones.
h. Which ones?

E.2

Add **one** *or* **ones** *where necessary.*

1. **A:** Which is your car?
   B: The blue ^one.
2. **A:** Do you want the black shoes?
   B: No, I prefer the brown.
3. **A:** Please bring that chair over here.
   B: The in the corner?
   A: Yes, please.
4. **A:** Do you need all the eggs?
   B: No, only the in the refrigerator.
   Give me two of them, please.
5. **A:** This apple is good.
   B: You're lucky. This is terrible.
6. **A:** Is there a supermarket near here?
   B: No, but there's about a mile away.
7. **A:** Which pills do you want?
   B: The on the kitchen table.
8. **A:** Do you want a hamburger?
   B: No, but Carla wants.
9. **A:** These cherries are good.
   B: The other are better.
10. **A:** Do you want these sandwiches?
    B: No, give me the over there.
11. **A:** I like this apartment.
    B: But the on Fifth Street costs less.
12. **A:** I want to buy some earrings.
    B: Do you want the gold earrings or the silver?

UNIT 7

Simple Present Tense and Present Progressive

A SIMPLE PRESENT TENSE AND PRESENT PROGRESSIVE: *HOW OFTEN;* QUESTIONS OF FREQUENCY; ADVERBS AND EXPRESSIONS OF FREQUENCY

A.1

Put a check (✓) next to the sentences that are true.

1. Americans almost always have dinner after nine o'clock. ______
2. Americans never celebrate birthdays. ______
3. Americans often give a present on a friend's or relative's birthday. ______
4. Americans rarely ski to work. ______
5. Americans always eat rice with dinner. ______
6. There are seldom fireworks on July 4th in the United States. ______
7. Americans don't usually drink tea at five o'clock in the afternoon. ______
8. Thanksgiving is always on Thursdays. ______
9. Americans sometimes work on Sundays. ______
10. Americans don't often drink coffee in the morning. ______

A.2

Write sentences with the logical adverbs or expressions of frequency.

1. The doctor says, "I go to the hospital."

   (rarely, usually) *I usually go to the hospital.*

2. The police officer says, "I arrest people."

   (sometimes, never) *I sometimes arrest people.*

3. The football player says, "I practice in the middle of the night."

   (always, rarely) ______________________

4. The salesperson says, "I fight with customers."

   (always, seldom) ______________________

5. The taxi driver says, "I drive at night."

   (never, often) ______________________________

6. The pharmacist says, "I'm careful."

   (always, rarely) ______________________________

7. The mechanic says, "I find the problem with the car."

   (almost always, seldom) ______________________________

8. The chef says, "I put lemon in milk."

   (never, often) ______________________________

9. The factory worker says, "I'm bored."

   (never, once in a while) ______________________________

10. The nurse says, "The hospital is open."

    (every day, frequently) ______________________________

11. The firefighter says, "I wear a suit and tie to work."

    (every day, almost never) ______________________________

12. The flight attendant says, "We're away from home for three or four days."

    (frequently, never) ______________________________

A.3

Write questions on the next page. Use **how often**. *Then answer the questions.*

	SWIM	PLAY BASKETBALL	DO EXERCISES	JOG
BARBARA	three times a week	never	every day	rarely
DONNA	once in a while	frequently	four times a week	five days a week
DAVID	never	almost every day	every morning	rarely
ED	once or twice a week	never	never	often
GEORGE	once or twice a week	almost every day	almost every day	almost never

(Continued on next page.)

1. (Barbara/do exercises)

How often does Barbara do exercises?

She does exercises every day.

2. (Donna/play basketball)

3. (David/swim)

4. (Barbara and Ed/play basketball)

5. (Ed/jog)

6. (Barbara/swim)

7. (Barbara and David/jog)

8. (Ed and George/swim)

9. (George and David/play basketball)

10. (George/jog)

____

____

11. (you/jog)

____

____

12. (you/do exercises)

____

____

A.4

Match the people with their activities.

1. __*i*__ artists	a. bake bread and cake
2. _____ bakers	b. count money
3. _____ bank tellers	c. cut meat
4. _____ bus drivers	d. do experiments
5. _____ butchers	e. drive buses
6. _____ doctors	f. examine patients
7. _____ gardeners	g. feed animals
8. _____ mechanics	h. fix cars
9. _____ newspaper reporters	i. paint pictures
10. _____ scientists	j. serve food
11. _____ waitresses	k. water plants and flowers
12. _____ zookeepers	l. write articles

A.5

Complete the sentences. Use the correct form of the verbs in exercise A.4.

1. Scott's a doctor. He *examines patients* every day. Right now he's in his office. He*'s examining a patient*.
2. Marilyn's a bus driver. She ________________ five days a week. Right now she's at work. She ________________.
3. Larry's a mechanic. Every day he ________________. Right now he's at his garage. He ________________.
4. Anne's a waitress. Every day she ________________. Right now she's at the restaurant. She ________________.
5. Sandra and Pat are artists. They ________________ almost every day. Right now they're both at their studios. They ________________.
6. Nicholas and Catherine are scientists. They ________________ every day. Right now they're in the lab. They ________________.
7. Renée and Cathy are newspaper reporters. They ________________ every afternoon. They're at work right now. They ________________.
8. Arthur's a butcher. He ________________ every day. Right now he's at his store. He ________________.
9. Linda's a bank teller. She ________________ all day long. Right now she's at the bank. She ________________.
10. Barry and Fred are bakers. They ________________ every morning. They're in the kitchen now. They ________________.
11. Ruth's a gardener. She ________________ almost every day. Right now she's at work. She ________________.
12. Jeffrey's a zookeeper. He ________________ two times a day. Right now he's in the elephant house. He ________________.

A.6

Complete the conversation. Use the correct form of the verbs in parentheses.

Marsha: Hello.

Alan: Hi, Marsha. This is Alan.

Marsha: Oh, hi, Alan.

Alan: What (you/do) ______________ (1.) right now? (you/do) ______________ (2.) anything important?

Marsha: No, I (cut) ______________ (3.) some vegetables for dinner. That's all.

Alan: (you/prepare) ______________ (4.) dinner at this time every evening?

Marsha: Yeah, usually. We (eat) ______________ (5.) at around 8:00. Why? When (you/have) ______________ (6.) dinner?

Alan: Oh, my family and I (eat) ______________ (7.) much earlier, probably because our kids (go) ______________ (8.) to bed by 7:30. In fact, they (get) ______________ (9.) ready for bed right now.

Marsha: Really? Our daughter (not go) ______________ (10.) to bed until 9:30, sometimes even ten o'clock. (your kids/go) ______________ (11.) to bed so early on the weekends, too?

Alan: No, but they (not stay up) ______________ (12.) later than 8:30. They (get up) ______________ (13.) at around 6:30 every morning, so they (be) ______________ (14.) tired by then. What (your daughter/do) ______________ (15.) all evening? (she/watch) ______________ (16.) a lot of television?

Marsha: No, she (practice) ______________ (17.) the violin. Actually, she (practice) ______________ (18.) right now.

Alan: How often (she/practice) ______________ (19.)?

Marsha: Every day for at least an hour.

Alan: You're kidding. (she/play) ______________ (20.) well?

Marsha: Very well. We (be) ______________ (21.) very proud of her.

(Continued on next page.)

Alan: I'm sure. Listen, I (work) ______________ (22.) on the report for the office, and there (be) ______________ (23.) a problem. (you/have) ______________ (24.) a couple of minutes to talk to me about it?

Marsha: Sure.

B NON-ACTION VERBS

B.1

Underline the verb in each sentence. Then write **action verb** *or* **non-action verb**.

1. I <u>have</u> a car. *non-action verb*
2. She <u>drives</u> badly. *action verb*
3. I don't have any brothers or sisters. ______________
4. Mitchell is having lunch. ______________
5. This book belongs to me. ______________
6. What do you need? ______________
7. Do you like horror movies? ______________
8. Do they come by bus every day? ______________
9. Do the flowers smell nice? ______________
10. Why are you smelling the meat? ______________
11. We do a lot of grammar exercises in this class. ______________
12. Why does he hate chocolate? ______________
13. I don't know the answer. ______________
14. Where are they running to? ______________

B.2

Complete the sentences. Circle the correct form of the verbs.

1. I ______________________ ten dollars. The money's in my bag.
   a. (have)
   b. am having

2. We ______________________ help. Let's ask the teacher.
   a. need
   b. are needing

3. I'm busy. I ______________________ on the phone.
   a. talk
   b. am talking

4. She ______________________ . Explain it to her again.
   a. does not understand
   b. is not understanding

5. Pedro ______________________ his family. That's why he's sad.
   a. misses
   b. is missing

6. You ______________________ in the right place. Look over there!
   a. do not look
   b. are not looking

7. There's a problem, but I ______________________ why.
   a. do not know
   b. am not knowing

8. I ______________________ . Don't talk to me!
   a. think
   b. am thinking

9. That shirt ______________________ good. Buy it!
   a. looks
   b. is looking

10. ______________________ that guy is nice?
    a. Do you think
    b. Are you thinking

11. There's a car outside. ______________________ to you?
    a. Does it belong
    b. Is it belonging

(Continued on next page.)

12. The little boy is unhappy. That's why he ______________________ .
    a. cries
    b. is crying

13. Let's stay. I ______________________ a good time.
    a. have
    b. am having

14. That music ______________________ terrible. Turn it off!
    a. sounds
    b. is sounding

B.3

Complete the sentences. Write the correct form of the verbs in parentheses.

A: What (you/want) ______________________ (1.) to do now?

B: I (not care) ______________________ (2.) . (you/want) ______________________ (3.) to go to the movies?

A: What (play) ______________________ (4.) ?

B: I (not know) ______________________ (5.) . I (not have) ______________________ (6.) a newspaper.

A: Well, let's go for a walk and get one.

B: But it (rain) ______________________ (7.) .

A: So what? I (have) ______________________ (8.) an umbrella.

B: But I (not have) ______________________ (9.) one.

A: Well, take mine. I (not need) ______________________ (10.) it. I (like) ______________________ (11.) the rain.

B: Okay.

A: Maybe Alex (want) ______________________ (12.) to come with us.

B: I (not think) ______________________ (13.) so. He (have) ______________________ (14.) a lot of homework tonight. He (do) ______________________ (15.) it right now.

A: But I (hear) ______________________ (16.) his voice. He (talk) ______________________ (17.) on the phone.

B: He (talk) ______________________ (18.) to a classmate. There's something he (not understand) ______________________ (19.) , and he (get) ______________________ (20.) some help.

A: How (you/know) ______________________ ?
21.

B: I (know) ______________________ everything.
22.

A: Well, you (not know) ______________________ what's on at the movies. So let's go!
23.

C VERB + NOUN OR INFINITIVE: *LIKE, PREFER, WANT, NEED*

C.1

Match the sentence with the speaker.

1. __d__ I want to clean the apartment. a. Pete
2. _____ All of you need to study more. b. Lulu
3. _____ My daughter-in-law does not like to take care of my son. c. Doug
4. _____ My daughter does not like to study very much. d. Yoko
5. _____ I prefer to wear sweatshirts. e. Carol
6. _____ I want to speak English perfectly. f. Norma
7. _____ I do not want to clean all the time. g. Yoko

C.2

Complete the sentences. Write the correct form of the verbs in the box.

be	buy	help	move	receive
relax	study	swim	talk	

1. **A:** Why are you going to the store?

   B: I want ___to buy___ some fruit.

2. **A:** Why do you go to the swimming pool on Sunday mornings?

   B: I prefer ______________ on Sundays. It's quiet then.

3. **A:** Why are you angry with your roommate?

   B: She never wants ______________ with the housework.

(Continued on next page.)

4. **A:** Why are you closing the door?

   B: I need ________________ to you in private.

5. **A:** Why are Gina and Louis looking for an apartment?

   B: They want ________________ .

6. **A:** Why are they going to the airport so late?

   B: They do not need ________________ at the airport until the evening.

7. **A:** Why do you write so many letters?

   B: Because we like ________________ them.

8. **A:** Why do you go to the library after class every day?

   B: I prefer ________________ there.

9. **A:** Why do you and your wife always stay home on Sundays?

   B: We like ________________ .

D POSSESSIVE ADJECTIVES AND POSSESSIVE PRONOUNS

D.1

Write **correct** *if the sentence is correct. Write* **car** *in the sentences where a noun is necessary*

1. Your is not working. *Your car is not working.*
2. Mine is not working. *correct*
3. Is this yours? ________________
4. Ours is over there. ________________
5. Please bring me my. ________________
6. Where is her? ________________
7. Give me hers, please. ________________
8. Theirs is on Park Street. ________________

9. We need our. ______________________________

10. Their is expensive. ______________________________

11. I like mine a lot. ______________________________

12. Why do you want your? ______________________________

D.2

Complete the sentences. Use **mine, his, hers, ours, yours,** *or* **theirs**.

1. I am not wearing her sweater. ___Hers___ is much smaller.
2. That's not my jacket. __________ is gray.
3. **A:** Is that his classroom?

   B: No, __________ is on the fifth floor.
4. **A:** Is that our suitcase?

   B: No, __________ is not light brown. We have a dark brown suitcase.
5. These are not your shoes. __________ are under the bed.
6. **A:** Is that their house?

   B: No, __________ is on Middle Street.
7. **A:** Are those your son's sneakers?

   B: No, __________ are a size 12.
8. **A:** Is that Ms. Gilman's office?

   B: No, __________ is in the next building.
9. They are not Yuri and Natasha's test papers. __________ are on my desk.
10. My roommate and I have a sofa like that one, but __________ is a little bigger.

D.3

Complete the conversation. Use the correct possessive adjective or possessive pronoun.

1. **A:** This is not ___my___ coat.

   B: Where's ___yours___?

   A: In the basement.

   B: Well, go and get it!

(Continued on next page.)

2. **A:** That's ____________ ball. Give it to me!

   B: No! It's not ____________ . It's ____________ . It's a birthday present from my brother.

3. **A:** Whose scarf is this?

   B: It's Nancy's.

   A: Are you sure it's ____________ ? This scarf is short, and she always wears long ones.

   B: I'm sure it's ____________ .

4. **A:** We're so happy with ____________ new car. We love it.

   B: You're lucky. We don't like ____________ at all. We always have a problem with it.

5. **A:** Do you know Bonnie and Tony Gray? ____________ son is on the football team.

   B: We know them, but we don't know ____________ son. Our son is on the junior high school team, but ____________ is on the high school team.

6. **A:** Is this your husband's hat?

   B: Yes, it is.

   A: How do you know it's ____________ ?

   B: Because all of ____________ hats have this mark.

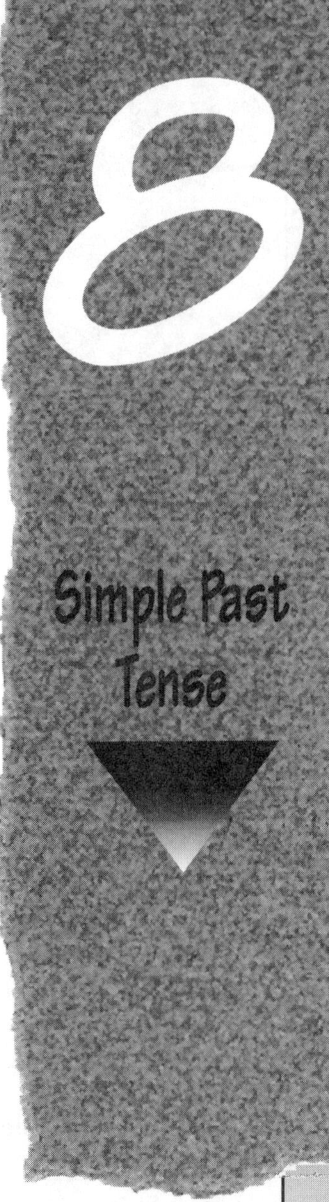

A SIMPLE PAST TENSE: REGULAR VERBS: AFFIRMATIVE AND NEGATIVE STATEMENTS

A.1

Match the situation with the best sentence.

1. __d__ Sylvia is tired.
2. ______ Sylvia's worried about her French test.
3. ______ Sylvia's car is clean.
4. ______ Sylvia is hungry.
5. ______ Sylvia's teacher is angry with her.
6. ______ Sylvia is happy.
7. ______ Sylvia's talking to a friend about a TV program.
8. ______ Sylvia feels bad.
9. ______ There's a lot of food in Sylvia's refrigerator.

a. She washed it yesterday.
b. Her boyfriend called her ten times yesterday to say, "I love you."
c. She watched it last night.
d. She didn't sleep much last night.
e. She didn't eat breakfast or lunch.
f. She didn't visit her grandparents.
g. She arrived late to class today.
h. She cooked a lot yesterday.
i. She didn't study very much.

A.2

Complete the sentences. Use **yesterday** *or* **last**.

Detective's Notes on Mr. Horace Smith	
April 15th	Traveled to Vancouver
April 25th	Borrowed $20,000
May 13th	Moved into a new apartment
(Nothing unusual until May 19th)	
May 19th	
7:00 A.M.	Arrived at work
2:00 P.M.	Finished work
6:00 P.M.	Returned to the office
11:00 P.M.	Visited someone at a hotel

It's Thursday, May 20th. Here's our report on Horace Smith.

____Last____ (1.) month he traveled to Vancouver. ________ (2.) month he also borrowed $20,000 from the bank. ________ (3.) week he moved into a new apartment. ________ (4.) morning he arrived at work at seven o'clock. At two o'clock ________ (5.) afternoon he finished work. Then something strange happened. He returned to the office at six o'clock ________ (6.) evening and visited someone at a hotel at eleven o'clock ________ (7.) night.

A.3

Answer the questions.

a. What day of the week is it today? ________

b. What month is it now? ________

c. What year is it now? ________

Use the answers above to rewrite the sentences. Use **ago**.

Example: Eric cleaned his apartment last Sunday. (It is Tuesday.)

Eric cleaned his apartment two days ago.

1. Eric traveled to Poland in 1991.

____

2. Eric visited his college roommate last July.

____

3. Eric called his parents last Monday.

____

4. Eric talked to his boss about a raise last Friday.

____

5. Eric graduated from college in 1988.

____

6. Eric moved to Georgia last December.

____

7. Eric played tennis last Thursday.

____

8. Eric studied Polish in 1989.

____

9. Eric's grandfather died last September.

____

A.4

Complete the sentences.

1. Pete walks to work every day.

   He walked to work _______ yesterday, too.

2. Lenny, Mike, and Warren play basketball every Saturday.

   _______________________ last Saturday, too.

(Continued on next page.)

3. Ellen washes her clothes every Sunday.

    ______________________________ last Sunday, too.

4. My classmates study every night.

    ______________________________ last night, too.

5. Robert works in his garden every weekend.

    ______________________________ last weekend, too.

6. Norma prepares dinner at 6:00 every day.

    ______________________________ yesterday, too.

7. Anna talks to her daughter every Friday night.

    ______________________________ last Friday night, too.

8. Michele and her husband travel to France every summer.

    ______________________________ last summer, too.

9. The bank closes at 3:00 P.M. every day.

    ______________________________ yesterday, too.

10. Adam and his sister watch television every night.

    ______________________________ last night, too.

A.5

Complete the sentences. Use the correct form of the verbs in parentheses.

1. I (wash) __________________ the clothes this morning, but I (not wash) __________________ the dishes.

2. We (invite) __________________ the Hangs to our party last week, but we (not invite) __________________ the Lees.

3. I (clean) __________________ the kitchen yesterday, but I (not clean) __________________ the bathroom.

4. Last night I (talk) __________________ to my aunt, but I (not talk) __________________ to my uncle.

5. I (call) __________________ your brother a few minutes ago, but I (not call) __________________ you.

6. We (watch) ________________ television last night, but we (not watch) ________________ the news.

7. Mr. Lugo (return) ________________ his book to the library today, but Mrs. Lugo (not return) ________________ hers.

8. The artist (paint) ________________ a picture of her sister, but she (not paint) ________________ a picture of her brother.

9. I (cook) ________________ some potatoes, but I (not cook) ________________ any meat.

10. I (study) ________________ history in high school, but I (not study) ________________ geography.

A.6

Complete the letter. Use the simple present tense, present progressive, or simple past tense of the verbs in parentheses.

April 12th

Dear Amira,

I (sit) ________________ (1.) at my desk, and I (think) ________________ (2.) of you. I often (think) ________________ (3.) of you on days like today. The sun (shine) ________________ (4.), and the birds (sing) ________________ (5.).

The weather's very different from the weather yesterday. It (rain) ________________ (6.) all day long and I (stay) ________________ (7.) in the house from morning until night. I (not go) ________________ (8.) out at all. I (wash) ________________ (9.) the clothes and (clean) ________________ (10.) the house—very exciting! After dinner I (play) ________________ (11.) cards with some neighbors.

One of my neighbors, Alfredo, (come) ________________ (12.) from Argentina. Sometimes I (speak) ________________ (13.) Spanish with him. I (not speak) ________________ (14.) Spanish very well, but Alfredo is very nice and never (laugh) ________________ (15.) at my mistakes.

Last week he (invite) ________________ (16.) me to an Argentinian party. We (listen) ________________ (17.) to beautiful music all night and I (dance) ________________ (18.) a lot. I really (enjoy) ________________ (19.) myself.

Well, it's time to go. I (cook) ________________ (20.) some Argentinian food, and I (need) ________________ (21.) to check it. I (not want) ________________ (22.) it to burn. You and I both (know) ________________ (23.) that I'm not a very good cook!

Write soon!

Love,

Connie

B SIMPLE PAST TENSE: IRREGULAR VERBS: AFFIRMATIVE AND NEGATIVE STATEMENTS

B.1

Underline the verb in each sentence. Write **regular** *if the simple past tense form is regular. Write* **irregular** *if the simple past tense form is irregular. Then write the base form of the verb.*

1. This morning I got up at seven o'clock. ___*irregular*___ ___*get*___
2. I washed my face and hands. ___*regular*___ ___*wash*___
3. Then I put on my clothes. ____________ ____________
4. I had orange juice and toast for breakfast. ____________ ____________
5. After breakfast I brushed my teeth. ____________ ____________
6. I left the house at 7:45. ____________ ____________
7. I arrived at school at 8:15. ____________ ____________
8. Class began at 8:30. ____________ ____________
9. We learned some new grammar rules in class today. ____________ ____________
10. Class finished at 11:30. ____________ ____________
11. I met some friends for lunch. ____________ ____________
12. We ate at a pizza place. ____________ ____________
13. After lunch we went to a swimming pool. ____________ ____________
14. We stayed there until four o'clock. ____________ ____________

B.2

Complete each sentence with the correct form of the verb.

1. I didn't eat eggs for breakfast. I ___*ate*___ cereal.
2. We didn't drink coffee. We ____________ tea.
3. He didn't leave at six o'clock. He ____________ at seven.
4. She didn't meet her sister at the movies. She ____________ her brother.
5. I didn't speak to the waiter. I ____________ to the manager.

(Continued on next page.)

6. I didn't go to the supermarket on Walnut Street. I ________________ to the supermarket on Chestnut Street.
7. The thief didn't steal my money. He ________________ my jewelry.
8. I didn't find your keys. I ________________ your address book.
9. We didn't drive to the park. We ________________ to the beach.
10. I didn't see Carol. I ________________ Yoko.
11. My husband didn't bring me flowers. He ________________ me chocolates.
12. We didn't come by bus. We ________________ by taxi.

B.3

Write true sentences.

1. I/become/an English teacher/last year

   I didn't become an English teacher last year.

2. I/eat/three kilos of oranges for breakfast/yesterday morning

   ____

3. I/sleep/twenty-one hours/yesterday

   ____

4. I/bring/a horse to English class/two weeks ago

   ____

5. I/go/to the moon/last month

   ____

6. I/meet/the leader of my country/last night

   ____

7. I/find/$10,000 in a brown paper bag/yesterday

   ____

8. I/do/this exercise/two years ago

   ____

9. I/swim/thirty kilometers/yesterday

____

10. I/speak/English perfectly/ten years ago

____

B.4

Complete the diary. Use the simple past tense form of the verbs in parentheses.

I (have) ________ (1.) a nice day today. I (not get) ________ (2.) up until ten o'clock, so I (get) ________ (3.) dressed quickly and (go) ________ (4.) to the Fine Arts Museum.

I (meet) ________ (5.) Cindy and Frank there, and we (go) ________ (6.) into the museum to see a new exhibit. We (not see) ________ (7.) everything because we (not have) ________ (8.) enough time. The exhibit (close) ________ (9.) at one o'clock. We (eat) ________ (10.) at a Chinese restaurant near the museum, and then we (take) ________ (11.) a bus to the Downtown Shopping Mall. We (stay) ________ (12.) at the mall for a couple of hours and (look) ________ (13.) around. I (buy) ________ (14.) a new shirt, but Frank and Cindy (not buy) ________ (15.) anything.

Cindy and Frank (come) ________ (16.) back home with me, and I (make) ________ (17.) dinner here. I (not have) ________ (18.) much in the refrigerator, so I (drive) ________ (19.) to the supermarket to get some things. I (see) ________ (20.) Ramon there and (invite) ________ (21.) him for dinner, too.

We (not eat) ________ (22.) until late, and after dinner we (watch) ________ (23.) a video. Ramon, Cindy, and Frank (not leave) ________ (24.) until after midnight.

It's one o'clock in the morning now, and I'm tired. It's time to go to bed. Good night!

C SIMPLE PAST TENSE: *YES/NO* QUESTIONS AND SHORT ANSWERS

C.1

Answer the questions. Use short answers. (Look at the conversation on page 206 of your grammar book if you need help.)

1. Did Carol have Thanksgiving dinner with her family?

   No, she didn't.

2. Did Carol and Yoko go to San Francisco for Thanksgiving?

   ____

3. Did Elenore make a turkey for Thanksgiving?

   ____

4. Did Pete prepare anything for the Thanksgiving dinner?

   ____

5. Did Norma have Thanksgiving dinner with her family?

   ____

6. Did Pete and Uncle Bob have a fight on Thanksgiving?

   ____

7. Did Uncle Bob like Pete's soup?

   ____

8. Did Pete and Elenore have Thanksgiving dinner at their home?

   ____

9. Did Uncle Bob watch a football game on television?

   ____

C.2

There's a mistake in each question. Write the question without the mistake.

1. You did finish the last exercise?
   Did you finish the last exercise?
2. Did you all the homework?
3. You did took a bath this morning?
4. Does your best friend come over to your house last night?
5. Did you went to bed early last night?
6. Did your English teacher taught you new grammar last week?
7. Do you visit the United States ten years ago?
8. Your mother and father got married a long time ago?
9. Did you watched television last night?

C.3

Answer the questions in exercise C.2. Use short answers.

1. (Did you finish the last exercise?)
   Yes, I did.
2. ______
3. ______
4. ______
5. ______
6. ______
7. ______
8. ______
9. ______

C.4

Look at Sharon's list. Write her husband's questions. Then complete each answer with the simple past tense form of the verbs in parentheses.

Things To Do

- Get the clothes from the dry cleaner's
- Buy food for dinner
- Meet Glen for lunch
- Write a letter to Rena
- Go to the bank
- Return the book to the library
- Look for a birthday present for Jane
- Call the doctor
- Bake some cookies
- Pick the children up at 4:00

Sharon: Steven, you always say I forget to do things. Well, today I remembered to do everything.

Steven: Are you sure? Let's see your list. *Did you get the clothes from the dry cleaner's?* (1.)

Sharon: Uh-huh. I (put) *put* (2.) them in the closet.

Steven: ____________________ (3.)

Sharon: Yes, I did. I (get) ________ (4.) some chicken, some vegetables, and some apples for dessert.

Steven: ____________________ (5.)

Sharon: Yeah. We (eat) ________ (6.) at a great Thai restaurant.

Steven: ____________________ (7.)

Sharon: Yes. I (mail) ________ (8.) it at the post office.

Steven: ____________________ (9.)

Sharon: Yes, I did. I (deposit) ________ (10.) both of the checks.

Steven: ____________________ (11.)

Sharon: Yes, I did. And I (take) ________ (12.) out another book by the same author.

Steven: ____
13.

Sharon: Yeah. I (buy) __________________ her a sweater.
14.

Steven: ____
15.

Sharon: Uh-huh. He (say) __________________ all the test results are fine.
16.

Steven: ____
17.

Sharon: Of course. And I (have) __________________ a few already. They're delicious.
18.

Steven: ____
19.

Sharon: Oh no, I (forget) __________________! What time is it?
20.

D SIMPLE PAST TENSE: *WH-* QUESTIONS

D.1

Match the questions and answers about Carol and Yoko's Thanksgiving holiday. (Be careful! There is one extra answer.)

1. __h__ Who drove from Oregon to San Francisco?	a. More than six hours.
2. ______ Where did Yoko and Carol rent the car?	b. Around Berkeley.
3. ______ When did Yoko and Carol arrive in San Francisco?	c. On Sunday.
	d. On Wednesday night.
4. ______ How long did it take to drive from Oregon to San Francisco?	e. Because they didn't bring their books.
	f. Because they didn't want to drive anymore.
5. ______ What did they do on Thursday?	g. Yoko's uncle.
6. ______ Where did they walk on Friday?	h. Yoko and Carol did.
7. ______ Who did they walk around Berkeley with?	i. They visited Fisherman's Wharf and Chinatown.
8. ______ Who invited Yoko and Carol to his home?	j. Yoko's friends.
9. ______ When did Carol write her grandmother?	k. In Oregon.
10. ______ Why didn't Carol and Yoko visit Yoko's uncle?	

D.2

Write questions. Then answer the questions. (If you need help, the answers are at the end of the exercise.)

1. Where/Americans/celebrate Thanksgiving/for the first time

   Where did Americans celebrate Thanksgiving for the first time?

   In Massachusetts.

2. When/a human being/walk on the moon/for the first time

3. What/William Shakespeare/write

4. Where/the Olympic games/start

5. Why/many people/go to California/in 1849

6. How long/John Kennedy/live in the White House

7. What/Alfred Hitchcock/make

8. Why/the Chinese/build the Great Wall

____

____

9. How long/World War II/last in Europe

____

____

10. When/Christopher Columbus/discover/America

____

____

Almost three years.	Movies.
About six years.	Plays like *Romeo and Juliet.*
In 1969.	They wanted to keep foreigners out of the country.
In 1492.	They wanted to find gold.
In Greece.	
In Massachusetts.	

D.3

Write questions. Use **who** *and the verb in parentheses.*

1. **A:** Carol went to San Francisco.

   B: (go) *Who did she go* with?

   A: With her roommate, Yoko.

   B: How did they go there?

   A: By car.

   B: (drive) *Who drove* ?

   A: I don't know. Probably both of them.

2. **A:** Those are beautiful flowers. (give) ______________ them to you?

   B: My boyfriend.

3. **A:** I went to a party at my old high school last night.

   B: (see) ______________ there?

(Continued on next page.)

4. **A:** You got a phone call a couple of minutes ago.

   B: (call) ______________________?

   A: A woman. Her name was Betty Kowalski.

5. **A:** Did you ever read the book *The Old Man and the Sea?*

   B: (write) ______________________ it?

   A: Ernest Hemingway.

6. **A:** Where are the children?

   B: At Ryan Santiago's house.

   A: (take) ______________________ them there?

   B: Ryan's mother.

7. **A:** My wife sent the money to your office a month ago.

   B: (send) ______________________ it to?

   A: Nicole Sanda.

8. **A:** The car is so clean. (clean) ______________________ it?

   B: I took it to a car wash.

   A: It looks great.

9. **A:** Did you hear the news? Kay got married.

   B: Really? (marry) ______________________?

   A: A guy from Oklahoma. I don't know his name.

10. **A:** My grandparents went to Arizona for two months last winter.

    B: (stay) ______________________ with?

    A: My cousin, Howard. He has a big house there.

D.4

Complete the conversation. Write questions. Use **what, where, when, who,** *or* **why**.

Police: There was a robbery last night, and someone said you did it.

Donald: That person's lying.

Police: Well, then. Tell us about your activities last night.

What did you do?
1.

Donald: We went to the movies.

Police: We? ______________________________
2.

Donald: A friend. Her name's Wendy Kaufman.

Police: ______________________________
3.

Donald: I left home at around 5:30.

Police: ______________________________
4.

Donald: The movie started at 8:30.

Police: ______________________________
5.

Donald: I left my house so early because we had dinner before the movie.

Police: ______________________________
6.

Donald: At Maxi's Steak House.

Police: ______________________________
7.

Donald: I met her at the restaurant.

Police: ______________________________
8.

Donald: A steak. That's what everybody eats at Maxi's.

Police: We're not interested in everybody. We're only interested in you.

____
9.

Donald: The waitress saw us, of course. And I talked to the manager, too.

Police: ______________________________
10.

Donald: Because the steak was no good.

Police: ______________________________
11.

Donald: After dinner? To the movies. I told you that already.

Police: ______________________________
12.

Donald: *Wine and Roses*. You know, the movie with Kristie McNeil.

Police: ______________________________
13.

Donald: At the Cinemax on Ocean Road.

UNIT

Past Tense of *Be*

A PAST TENSE OF *BE*: AFFIRMATIVE AND NEGATIVE STATEMENTS, *YES/NO* QUESTIONS, AND SHORT ANSWERS

A.1

Kim went shopping at Miller's Department Store. Complete the sentences about her purchases. Use **was** *or* **were**.

1. *The pants were $45.*
2. *The jacket was $79.99.*
3. ______________________
4. ______________________
5. ______________________
6. ______________________
7. ______________________
8. ______________________
9. ______________________
10. ______________________
11. ______________________
12. ______________________

Pants	$45.00
Jacket	$79.99
Shirt	$29.99
Tie	$16.00
Socks	$8.00
Sweater	$39.00
Coat	$145.00
Pajamas	$19.99
Shorts	$14.99
Gloves	$25.00
Hat	$22.00
Shoes	$65.00

A.2

Write sentences. Use **was, wasn't, were,** *or* **weren't.**

1. Abraham Lincoln/born/in England

   Abraham Lincoln wasn't born in England.

2. Picasso and Michelangelo/painters

   Picasso and Michelangelo were painters.

3. William Shakespeare and Charles Dickens/Canadian

____

4. Ronald Reagan/the first president of the United States

____

5. Charlie Chaplin and Marilyn Monroe/movie stars

____

6. The end of World War I/in 1922

____

7. *E.T.*/ the name of a movie

____

8. Toronto and Washington, D.C./big cities 300 years ago

____

9. Indira Gandhi and Napoleon/famous people

____

10. Margaret Thatcher/a political leader

____

11. Oregon and Hawaii/part of the United States/in 1776

____

12. Disneyland/a famous place/100 years ago

____

A.3

Answer the questions. Use short answers.

1. Was Carol with her family on Thanksgiving? *No, she wasn't.*
2. Were your parents born in New York? _______________
3. Were you a happy child? _______________
4. Was your father a good student? _______________
5. Was it cold yesterday? _______________
6. Were you born in a hospital? _______________

Now answer these questions.

7. Was Yoko with Carol on Thanksgiving? *Yes, she was.*
8. Did Carol and Yoko go to New York for Thanksgiving? *No, they didn't.*
9. Were you and a friend at the movies last night? ______
10. Did you buy anything yesterday? ______
11. Was the last grammar exercise easy? ______
12. Did you take a shower yesterday? ______
13. Did your English teacher give you a test last week? ______
14. Were you absent from your last English class? ______
15. Did your parents get married five years ago? ______

A.4

Write questions and answers. Use the past tense of **be**.

1. **A:** We had a nice holiday.

   B: (you/with your whole family) *Were you with your whole family?*

   A: (no/my daughter/in Montreal) *No, my daughter was in Montreal.*

2. **A:** I bought these new shoes yesterday.

   B: (they/on sale) ______

   A: (yes/they/only $25) ______

3. **A:** (you/at home/last night) ______

   B: (no/I/at the library) ______

4. **A:** (the guests/late for the party) ______

   B: (no/they/all on time) ______

5. **A:** (it/warm/in Australia) ______

   B: (the weather/beautiful/every day) ______

6. **A:** (the movie/good) ______

   B: (it/okay) ______

7. **A:** (the people at the party/friendly) ______________________________

   B: (most of them/very nice) ______________________________

8. **A:** I called the lawyer.

   B: (he/there) ______________________________

   A: (no/he/at a meeting) ______________________________

A.5

Complete the conversation. Use **is, are, was,** *or* **were.**

A: It ___*is*___ (1.) a beautiful day. The sun feels so good.

B: Yes, it does—especially because the weather ___*was*___ (2.) so terrible yesterday. The weather in this city __________ (3.) so strange. One day it __________ (4.) warm, and the next day it __________ (5.) cold.

A: You __________ (6.) right about that. In my country, it __________ (7.) always warm and sunny.

B: __________ (8.) warm in the winter, too?

A: Uh-huh. It __________ (9.) rarely colder than 70 degrees. This last Christmas I __________ (10.) home for two weeks, and it __________ (11.) sunny and warm. My friends and I __________ (12.) at the beach every day. How about you? __________ (13.) you here this past Christmas?

B: Yeah. My parents __________ (14.) here for a few days for a visit. We __________ (15.) cold most of the time, and my mother __________ (16.) ill for a few days. They __________ (17.) happy to see me, but they __________ (18.) glad to leave this awful weather.

A: __________ (19.) your parents back home now?

B: No, they __________ (20.) on another vacation—this time, in a warm place.

B PAST TENSE OF *BE*: *WH-* QUESTIONS

B.1

Complete the conversations. Choose the correct question.

1. **A:** I was absent yesterday.

   B: *What was wrong?*

   a. Who was absent?
   b. What was wrong?

   A: I was ill.

2. **A:** We had dinner at the new Mexican restaurant.

   B: ______________________________

   a. How was the food?
   b. Where was the restaurant?

   A: Very good.

3. **A:** You forgot Cathy's birthday.

   B: ______________________________

   a. When was it?
   b. Where was she?

   A: Last Thursday.

4. **A:** I went to bed at eight o'clock last night.

   B: ______________________________

   a. What did you do?
   b. Why were you so tired?

   A: I don't know. I didn't feel very well.

5. **A:** You missed a great party.

   B: ______________________________

   a. Who was there?
   b. How was the party?

   A: People from our class and their friends.

6. **A:** I found your keys.

   B: ____

   a. Where were they?
   b. Why were they there?

   A: Under the desk.

7. **A:** I got everything right on the test.

   B: ____

   a. Really? Where were the answers to the first and third questions?
   b. Really? What were the answers to the first and third questions?

   A: The answer to the first was C, and D was the answer to the third.

8. **A:** We were on vacation for two weeks.

   B: ____

   a. Why were you on vacation?
   b. How was it?

   A: It was great.

9. **A:** We had a great time in Hong Kong.

   B: ____

   a. Who were you with?
   b. When were you there?

   A: We were there about two years ago.

B.2

Complete the questions. Use **was, were,** *or* **did**.

1. Why ____________ you go there?
2. Who ____________ you with?
3. What ____________ you wear?
4. How ____________ the weather?
5. Where ____________ you yesterday?
6. How ____________ you get to the beach?
7. Where ____________ your husband?
8. When ____________ he come home?

9. What __________ the problem with the bus?

10. Why __________ he angry?

11. Where __________ your friends meet you?

12. Why __________ your friends late?

B.3

Here are the answers to the questions in exercise B.2. Match the questions and answers.

1. Where were you yesterday? — At the beach.
2. __________ — It was beautiful.
3. __________ — By bus.
4. __________ — It was crowded.
5. __________ — We wanted to swim.
6. __________ — Some friends.
7. __________ — At the bus station.
8. __________ — They woke up late.
9. __________ — My new bathing suit.
10. __________ — At his office.
11. __________ — He didn't go to the beach with us.
12. __________ — Late last night.

B.4

Complete the conversations. Write the correct questions. Use **was** *or* **were**.

1. **A:** Did you pay a lot of money for those sunglasses?

   B: No, they were on sale.

   A: When were they on sale?

   B: Last week.

2. **A:** I tried to call you last night.

   B: I wasn't home.

   A: Where __________?

   B: At a friend's apartment.

3. **A:** Did you have your history test yesterday?

   B: No, we had it today.

   A: How ______________________________ ?

   B: It was okay, but I didn't know the answers to two of the questions.

4. **A:** Did the kids go swimming?

   B: No, they were afraid.

   A: Why ______________________________ ?

   B: The water was deep.

5. **A:** Did you go to the basketball game?

   B: Yeah, it was a great game.

   A: What ______________________________ ?

   B: I don't remember the score, but our team won.

6. **A:** Those are beautiful shoes. Where did you get them?

   B: At a store on Washington Street.

   A: What ______________________________ ?

   B: I think the name of the store was Dalton's. Or, was it Dillon's?

7. **A:** Did your dog have her puppies yet?

   B: She sure did—six of them.

   A: When ______________________________ ?

   B: They were born a few days ago.

8. **A:** What's new?

   B: The police were here.

   A: Why ______________________________ ?

   B: Someone called them, but I don't know why.

9. **A:** You were brave to go there alone.

   B: I wasn't alone.

   A: Who ______________________________ ?

   B: My brother and sister.

10. **A:** Did you ever read this book?

    B: Yes, it was about Eleanor Roosevelt.

    A: Who ______________________________ ?

    B: She was the wife of President Roosevelt.

11. **A:** Do you know this school, the Foreign Language Institute?

    B: Yes, I took a couple of German classes there last year.

    A: How ______________________________ ?

    B: Both of my teachers were very good.

C PAST OF *BE*: *THERE WAS/THERE WERE*

C.1

Put a check (✓) next to the statements that are true.

In the eighteenth century:

1. There weren't any televisions. ______
2. There weren't any horses. ______
3. There were houses. ______
4. There wasn't any water. ______
5. There were radios. ______
6. There was a war. ______
7. There weren't any car accidents. ______

8. There weren't any pianos. ______

9. There was cold weather. ______

10. There were telephones. ______

C.2

Do you remember Unit 2 of your grammar book? Complete the description. Use **there was** *or* **there were**.

1. ____________________ a picture of a man at an eye doctor's office.
2. ____________________ some grammar exercises.
3. ____________________ a conversation between Lulu and a woman at a laundromat.
4. ____________________ a letter from Carol to her grandmother.
5. ____________________ grammar notes.
6. ____________________ two pictures of desks.
7. ____________________ a story.
8. ____________________ many questions.
9. ____________________ lots of things to do.
10. ____________________ a description of Carol's family.

C.3

Complete the sentences about the newspaper headlines. Use **there was, there wasn't, there were,** *or* **there weren't.**

PLANE CRASH KILLS TWO

Bank Robbery At Freedom Savings
Two robbers get away with $50,000
Lorem ipsum dolor sit amet, consectetuer adipiscing elit, sed diam nonummy nibh euismod tincidunt ut laoreet dolore magna aliquam erat volutpat. Ut wis quis nostrud ex suscipit loborti ullamcorper su nibh euismod ti magna aliquam enim ad minin exerci tation ulla

No Classes At Norton Community College
Fight between students

• FIRE AT CENTRAL ELEMENTARY SCHOOL •
NO INJURIES REPORTED

Car Accident Injures Five

NO BASEBALL GAMES YESTERDAY
Players' one-day strike is over

MEETING BETWEEN LEADERS OF THE U.S. AND CHINA
Discussions about many important problems

Earthquake In British Columbia
No reports of deaths or injuries

1. *There was* ________ a plane crash. *There were* ________ two deaths.
2. ________ a fire at Central Elementary School. ________ any injuries.
3. ________ a bank robbery at Freedom Savings Bank. ________ two robbers.
4. ________ a car accident. ________ five injuries.
5. ________ any classes at Norton Community College because ________ a fight between students.
6. ________ a meeting between the leaders of the United States and China. ________ discussions about many important problems.
7. ________ an earthquake in British Columbia, but ________ any reports of deaths or injuries.
8. ________ any baseball games yesterday. ________ a strike.

C.4

Answer the questions. Use short answers.

1. Was there a fire near your home yesterday? ____________________
2. Were there enough chairs for everyone in your last English class? ____________________
3. Was there a good program on TV last night? ____________________
4. Was there a break during your last English class? ____________________
5. Were there any visitors at your home late last night? ____________________
6. Were there any problems in your town last week? ____________________
7. Was there a test in your English class last week? ____________________
8. Were there any letters in the mail for you last week? ____________________

C.5

Complete the conversation. Write questions. Use the words in the box.

cheap restaurants?	a casino on the island?
a view of the sea from your hotel room?	many places to go shopping?
a lot of tourists?	many English-speaking people?
interesting things to see?	a beach near the hotel?
a restaurant in the hotel?	

A: I hear you went to the Caribbean for your vacation.

B: Yes, we did. It was wonderful.

A: *Were there a lot of tourists?*
1.

B: No, we were surprised. There weren't many people at all.

A: How was your hotel?

B: It wasn't bad. It was on the sea and it wasn't too expensive.

A: ____________________
2.

B: Yes, it was beautiful. It was nice to wake up in the morning and see hundreds of boats outside our window.

A: ____________________
3.

B: Yes, we had breakfast there every morning.

A: ____
4.

B: Yes, but it wasn't very clean. We never went swimming there.

A: ____
5.

B: Uh-huh. We never spent too much money on lunch or dinner.

A: ____
6.

B: Yes. We went somewhere different every day.

A: ____
7.

B: There were a few tourist shops near the big hotels. They had postcards, T-shirts—things like that.

A: ____
8.

B: No, there weren't. Most of the people spoke only French.

A: ____
9.

B: I don't know. We don't like to gamble, and we always went to bed early.

A COUNT AND NON-COUNT NOUNS AND QUANTIFIERS

A.1

Look at the store signs. Write the correct aisle number.

Aisle	Items	Aisle	Items	Aisle	Items
1	Eggs, Butter, Juice, Cheese, Milk		Toilet Paper, Paper Towels, Napkins, Plastic Bags		Frozen Food, Ice Cream
	Bread, Rolls		Potato Chips, Cookies, Cereal		Canned Vegetables, Canned Fish, Rice
	Toothbrushes, Toothpaste, Soap, Shampoo		Sugar, Flour, Salt		Fresh Fruit

1. Sugar is in aisle __6__.
2. Cookies are in aisle ______.
3. Ice cream is in aisle ______.
4. Eggs are in aisle ______.
5. Fruit is in aisle ______.
6. Canned vegetables are in aisle ______.
7. Napkins are in aisle ______.
8. Milk is in aisle ______.
9. Rice is in aisle ______.
10. Plastic bags are in aisle ______.
11. Potato chips are in aisle ______.
12. Frozen food is in aisle ______.
13. Bread is in aisle ______.
14. Canned fish is in aisle ______.
15. Toothbrushes are in aisle ______.

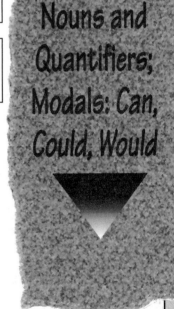

A.2

Write the underlined words in exercise A.1 in the correct column.

COUNT NOUNS	NON-COUNT NOUNS
cookies	*sugar*

A.3

Find the twelve mistakes in the list of count nouns and non-count nouns. Circle them. Then write the list again. Write **a, an,** *or* **some** *before each word.*

COUNT NOUNS	NON-COUNT NOUNS	COUNT NOUNS	NON-COUNT NOUNS
egg	books	*an egg*	*some bread*
(bread)	food	*some books*	*some food*
furniture	water	______	______
student	people	______	______
money	paper	______	______
information	uncle	______	______
teeth	homework	______	______
rain	advice	______	______
children	television	______	______
friends	traffic	______	______
oil	questions	______	______
animal	computer	______	______

A.4

Complete the sentences. Choose the correct words.

1. Do you have ______ a pencil ______?
   a. some pencil
   b. a pencil

2. The ______________________ on the table.
   a. money is
   b. money are

3. There ______________________ in the refrigerator.
   a. is some fruit
   b. are some fruits

4. We don't have ______________________.
   a. much book
   b. many books

5. Do you want ______________________?
   a. an apple
   b. some apple

6. I'm sorry I'm late. The ______________________ terrible.
   a. traffic was
   b. traffics were

7. Do you like Chinese ______________________?
   a. food
   b. foods

8. Do you have ______________________?
   a. a water
   b. any water

9. Is there ______________________ in the bedroom?
   a. a radio
   b. any radio

10. Don't rush! We have a lot of ______________________.
    a. time
    b. times

11. I want ______________________.
    a. an information
    b. some information

A.5

Jack did some Sunday morning shopping. He brought some things on his shopping list, but he didn't buy everything. Write sentences about what he bought and about what he did not buy. Use **some, any,** *or* **a**.

Shopping List

~~Bananas~~	Toothbrush
Cheese	~~Potatoes~~
~~Orange juice~~	Lettuce
Lemons	Carrots
~~Newspaper~~	~~Butter~~
Bread	~~Milk~~
Onions	~~Eggs~~

1. *He bought some bananas.* ________________
2. *He didn't buy any cheese.* ________________
3. ________________________________
4. ________________________________
5. ________________________________
6. ________________________________
7. ________________________________
8. ________________________________
9. ________________________________
10. ________________________________
11. ________________________________
12. ________________________________
13. ________________________________
14. ________________________________

A.6

Write ten true sentences. Use words from each column.

<table>
<tr><td>I have</td><td>a lot of
a little
a few</td><td rowspan="2">cheese in my pocket
food in my refrigerator
money in my pocket
books next to my bed
shirts in my closet
friends
free time
children
work to do today
questions for my teacher
jewelry
medicine in my bathroom
problems with English grammar
photographs in my wallet
ice cream at home</td></tr>
<tr><td>I don't have</td><td>much
many
any</td></tr>
</table>

Example: *I don't have any cheese in my pocket.*

1. ______________________________

2. ______________________________

3. ______________________________

4. ______________________________

5. ______________________________

6. ______________________________

7. ______________________________

8. ______________________________

9. ______________________________

10. ______________________________

B COUNT AND NON-COUNT NOUNS: *YES/NO* QUESTIONS; QUESTIONS ABOUT QUANTITY: *HOW MUCH* AND *HOW MANY*

B.1

Match the containers and non-count nouns.

1. a can of	a. lettuce
2. a carton of	b. soda
3. a head of	c. bread
4. a loaf of	d. milk

Do the same with these words.

5. a bottle of	e. cake
6. a box of	f. cigarettes
7. a pack of	g. juice
8. a piece of	h. cereal

Do the same with these words, too.

9. a bar of	i. toothpaste
10. a jar of	j. toilet paper
11. a roll of	k. jam
12. a tube of	l. soap

B.2

Look at Tina's cash register receipt and answer the questions.

1. How much soda did she buy?

   Six cans

2. How many loaves of bread did she buy?

   One

3. How much milk did she buy?

   ______

6 Soda	**$2.19**
1 Bread	**$1.05**
1 Milk	**$1.19**
2 Lettuce	**$3.58**
3 Apple juice	**$5.40**
1 Cereal	**$2.29**
4 Toilet paper	**$1.69**
3 Soap	**$2.45**
1 Toothpaste	**$2.39**
2 Jam	**$3.38**
TOTAL	**$25.61**

THANK YOU FOR SHOPPING
AT CASTLE'S

4. How much lettuce did she buy?

____

5. How many bottles of apple juice did she buy?

____

6. How many boxes of cereal did she buy?

____

7. How much toilet paper did she buy?

____

8. How much soap did she buy?

____

9. How much toothpaste did she buy?

____

10. How many jars of jam did she buy?

____

B.3

Write questions. Use **a, an,** *or* **any**.

1. telephone/in your bedroom

   Is there a telephone in your bedroom?

2. flowers/in a vase in your home

   Are there any flowers in a vase in your home?

3. trash/in your kitchen

   Is there any trash in your kitchen?

4. furniture/in your home

   ____

5. clothes/in your closet

   ____

6. money/under your bed

   ____

7. alarm clock/next to your bed

____

8. snow/on the ground outside your home

____

9. sink/in your bathroom

____

10. dishes/in your kitchen sink

____

11. pictures/on the walls of your bedroom

____

12. candy/in your home

____

13. window/in your kitchen

____

14. television/in your living room

____

B.4

Answer the questions in exercise B.3. Use short answers.

1. _______________
2. _______________
3. _______________
4. _______________
5. _______________
6. _______________
7. _______________
8. _______________
9. _______________
10. _______________

11. ____________________

12. ____________________

13. ____________________

14. ____________________

B.5

Write questions. Use **how many** *or* **how much**.

A: Are you going to the store?

B: Yes, why?

A: I need some things. I need some cheese.

B: *How much cheese do you need?*
1.

A: About a pound. And I want some eggs.

B: *How many eggs do you want?*
2.

A: A dozen. I also need some flour.

B: ____________________
3.

A: One pound, I think.

B: Do you want any sugar?

A: No, I have sugar.

B: ____________________
4.

A: A few cups, at least. But I want some bananas.

B: ____________________
5.

A: Five or six. I want some oranges, too.

B: ____________________
6.

A: A few. Oh, and I need some rice.

B: ____________________
7.

A: A box. I also need some potatoes.

B: ____________________
8.

A: Get about ten. Oh, one more thing. I want some milk.

B: ____________________
9.

(Continued on next page.)

A: Half a gallon. Oh, don't forget to get some flowers. I want roses.

B: ______________________________ 10.

A: Half a dozen.

B: Is that it? Are you sure you don't want any cookies?

A: No, I have enough cookies.

B: ______________________________ 11.

A: Two dozen. Here, let me give you some money.

B: I have money.

A: ______________________________ 12.

B: About twenty dollars.

A: Here. Take another twenty.

C *ENOUGH* + NOUN; *TOO MUCH/TOO MANY/ TOO LITTLE/TOO FEW* + NOUN

C.1

Complete the sentences. Choose the correct words.

1. What did the student say to the teacher?

   "I didn't finish the homework. I *didn't have enough* time."

   a. had too much

   b. didn't have enough

2. What did the driver say to the passenger in her car?

   "We ______________ gas. We need to go to the gas station."

   a. have too much

   b. don't have enough

3. What did the passenger in the car say to the driver?

   "There ______________ cars. Let's go to another parking lot."

   a. are too many

   b. aren't enough

4. What did the cashier at the drugstore say to the little girl?

   "I'm sorry. You have ______________________ money. Go home and get some more."
   a. too much
   b. too little

5. Ted and Niki wanted to see a movie, but there was a long line for tickets. What did Ted say?

   "There are ______________________ people. Let's go and see another movie."
   a. too many
   b. too few

6. What did the doctor say to his patient?

   "You said you're on a diet, but you lost only one pound last month. That

   ______________________ weight."
   a. is too much
   b. isn't enough

7. What did the photography teacher say to the student?

   "This picture is dark. You had ______________________ light."
   a. too much
   b. too little

8. What did Mitchell's mother say to him?

   "You ate ______________________ fruit. That's why you have a stomachache."
   a. too much
   b. too little

9. What did the customer say to the waitress?

   "There are ______________________ forks on the table for six people.
   a. too many
   b. too few

   Please bring some more."

10. What did Debbie say to her roommate?

    "You bought ______________________ juice. There's no place to put all
    a. too much
    b. too little

    these bottles."

C.2

Write sentences about the pictures. Use **not enough, too much,** *or* **too many** *and the words in the box.*

air	birds	days	furniture	people	toothpaste
batteries	chairs	food	numbers	shampoo	water

1.

There are too many people in the boat.

2.

FEBRUARY						
S	M	T	W	T	F	S
1	2	3	4	5	6	7
8	9	10	11	12	13	14
15	16	17	18	19	20	21
22	23	24	25	26	27	28
29	30	31				

3.

4.

5.

6.

7.

8.

9.

10.

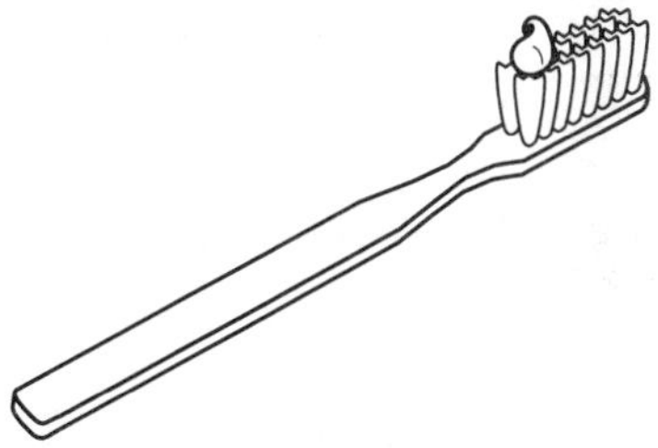

11.

12.

______________________ ______________________ ______________________

______________________ ______________________ ______________________

C.3

Rewrite the sentences. Use **too little** *or* **too few.**

1. We don't have enough chairs.

   We have too few chairs.

2. There isn't enough salt in this soup.

   There's too little salt in this soup.

3. There weren't enough people for two teams.

   ____

4. We didn't have enough paper for everyone in the class.

   ____

5. There wasn't enough food for fifteen people.

   ____

6. You don't have enough information.

   ____

7. There aren't enough bedrooms in that apartment.

   ____

8. We didn't have enough time for the test.

   ____

(Continued on next page.)

9. These aren't enough bananas for a banana cake.

____

10. There aren't enough salespeople at that store.

____

D MODALS: *CAN* AND *COULD* FOR ABILITY AND POSSIBILITY; *MAY I, CAN I,* AND *COULD I* FOR POLITE REQUESTS

D.1

Look at the job advertisements and the qualifications of Martha, Frank, Les, and Rosa. Then answer the questions.

WANTED
SECRETARY
Type 70 words per minute.
Need to speak Spanish.

WANTED
•SUMMER BABYSITTER•
Take two small children to the beach every day.
Also, go horseback riding with ten-year-old girl.

DRIVER WANTED
Drive truck to airport every day. Pick up boxes and deliver to downtown offices.

WANTED
SUMMER CAMP WORKER
◆ Teach children the guitar.
◆ Also work with children in art class

	MARTHA	FRANK	LES	ROSA
draw	no	no	yes	yes
drive	yes	no	yes	no
lift 100 pounds	no	no	yes	yes
play the guitar	no	yes	no	yes
ride a horse	yes	no	no	no
speak Spanish	no	yes	no	yes
swim	yes	yes	no	yes
type	yes	yes	no	no

1. Which job is good for Martha? The job as *summer babysitter*
2. Which job is good for Frank? The job as ______________________
3. Which job is good for Les? The job as ______________________
4. Which job is good for Rosa? The job as ______________________

D.2

Look at the information in exercise D.1 again. Then answer the questions. Use **can** *or* **can't.**

1. Why is the job as babysitter good for Martha?

   She *can swim and ride a horse.*

2. Why isn't the job as babysitter good for Rosa?

   She *can swim, but she can't ride a horse.*

3. Why isn't the job as babysitter good for Les?

   He *can't swim, and he can't ride a horse.*

4. Why is the job as driver good for Les?

   He ______________________________

5. Why is the job as secretary good for Frank?

   He ______________________________

6. Why is the job as summer camp worker good for Rosa?

   She ______________________________

7. Why isn't the job as driver good for Frank?

   ____

8. Why isn't the job as secretary good for Martha?

   ____

9. Why isn't the job as driver good for Rosa?

   ____

10. Why isn't the job as summer camp worker good for Les?

    ____

11. Why isn't the job as summer camp worker good for Martha?

    ____

12. Why isn't the job as secretary good for Les?

    ____

D.3

Write questions. Use **can.**

1. you/drive Can you drive?
2. your mother/lift 100 pounds ______
3. your father/play the guitar ______
4. your best friend/ride a horse ______
5. your parents/speak Spanish ______
6. you/swim ______
7. you/type ______

D.4

Answer the questions in exercise D.3. Use short answers.

1. ______
2. ______
3. ______
4. ______
5. ______
6. ______
7. ______

D.5

Complete the sentences. Use **could** *or* **couldn't** *and the verbs in parentheses.*

1. I'm sorry that I (call) couldn't call you yesterday. I was very busy.
2. We enjoyed our holiday in Spain because we (practice) ______ our Spanish.
3. We (go) ______ to the party last night. Our son was ill.
4. I didn't answer the questions. I (understand) ______ the story.
5. I had a terrible stomachache yesterday. I (eat) ______ a thing.
6. In high school I had a lot of free time. I (play) ______ soccer with my friends every Saturday and Sunday.

7. We didn't meet our friends for dinner last night. We (find) ________________ the restaurant.
8. Our room in that hotel was terrible. We (hear) ________________ the people in the other room all the time.
9. We don't have photographs from the museum. It was dark and we (use) ________________ a flash.
10. I liked my summer job. I (do) ________________ what I wanted.

D.6

Make polite requests. Use **may I** *or* **can I**.

1. You have a doctor's appointment at four o'clock. You want to leave early because class finishes at four o'clock. Ask your teacher.

   Can I leave class early? (OR: May I leave class early?)
2. You're in a friend's room. You're hot and you want to open the window. Ask your friend.

   ____
3. You're in an office. You want to use the telephone on the secretary's desk. Ask the secretary.

   ____
4. You're in your car and see a classmate at a bus stop. You want to give her a ride. Ask your classmate.

   ____
5. You're in class. You made a mistake, but you don't have an eraser. Your classmate has an eraser. Ask your classmate.

   ____
6. You're at your neighbor's house. You want to have a drink of water. Ask your neighbor.

   ____
7. You don't understand something in your grammar book. You want to ask your teacher a question.

   ____
8. You're at a restaurant. You want to sit at the empty table in the corner. Ask the waiter.

   ____

E DESIRES, INVITATIONS, AND POLITE REQUESTS: *WOULD LIKE, WOULD YOU LIKE, WOULD YOU PLEASE, COULD YOU PLEASE*

E.1

Read the conversations. Then answer the questions.

CONVERSATION A

A: Can I help you?

B: Yes, I'd like two tickets to Pittsburgh.

A: Would you like one-way or round-trip?

B: Round-trip, please.

A: That's $38.90.

B: Here you are. What time is the next bus?

A: At 9:30.

B: Thank you.

CONVERSATION B

A: Sir, would you like chicken or fish?

B: Chicken, please.

A: And what would you like to drink?

B: Just some water, please.

A: And your wife?

B: She doesn't want anything. She doesn't like airplane food.

CONVERSATION C

A: Where would you like to sit?

B: These seats are fine. I don't want to sit too close to the screen.

A: Would you like some popcorn?

B: No, but I'd like something to drink. But hurry! The movie's going to start.

1. Where does conversation A take place? ______________________
2. Where does conversation B take place? ______________________
3. Where does conversation C take place? ______________________

E.2

Rewrite the sentences. Use **would like**.

1. I want two airmail stamps.

   I would like two airmail stamps.

2. Do you want to have dinner with me?

   ____

3. Sheila wants to talk to you.

   ____

4. Do your parents want to come?

   ____

5. Sandy and Billy want some coffee.

   ____

6. Does Dan want to come with us?

   ____

7. My friend and I want a table for two.

   ____

8. Does the teacher want to come to the party?

   ____

9. I want to take a long trip.

   ____

10. We want you to have dinner with us.

    ____

E.3

Ari is making plans for a surprise birthday party for his roommate, Tony. He needs help from his friends. Look at his list. Write sentences. Use **would like**.

Surprise Birthday Party

1. Jerry — do some of the shopping
2. Conchita — bring the CDs
3. Irene and Amira — help with the cooking
4. Eric — bring his CD player
5. Harry, Mike, and Tom — move the furniture
6. Ellen — buy some ice cream
7. Victor — pick up the birthday cake
8. Carmen and Ted — keep Tony busy
9. Ratana — make the decorations

1. *Ari would like Jerry to do some of the shopping.*
2. ______________________________
3. ______________________________
4. ______________________________
5. ______________________________
6. ______________________________
7. ______________________________
8. ______________________________
9. ______________________________

E.4

Complete the conversation. Use the words in parentheses.

Dave: Hi, Ellen. Come on in.

Ellen: Hi, Dave. Thanks.

Dave: (you/ like) ___Would you like___ some coffee?
1.

Ellen: Yes. That sounds good. (you/ like) ______________ some help?
2.

Dave: No, it's ready. Here you are.

Ellen: Thanks.

Dave: (you/ like) ______________ some cookies, too?
3.

Ellen: No, thanks, but I (like) ______________ some sugar.
4.

Dave: Oh, sorry. I forgot. Here's the sugar.

Ellen: Boy, it's cold outside.

Dave: (you/ like/me/give) ______________ you a sweater?
5.

Ellen: No, I'm okay.

Dave: So, (what/you/ like/do) ______________ this evening?
6.

Ellen: I don't know. (Where/you/ like/go) ______________?
7.

Dave: (you/ like/go) ______________ to the movies?
8.

Ellen: What's playing?

Dave: *Forever Love* is at the Rex. (you/ like/see) ______________ that?
9.

Ellen: Okay. What time does it start?

Dave: We can go at six, eight, or ten.

Ellen: I don't care. (What time/you/like/go) ______________?
10.

Dave: Eight is fine, but I (like/get) ______________ something to eat before.
11.

Ellen: Okay. (Where/ you/like/eat) ______________?
12.

Dave: How about John's Pizzeria?

Ellen: That sounds good.

E.5

Write the correct question. Use **would you** *or* **could you**.

1. Ask a stranger on the bus to tell you the time.

   Would you please tell me the time? (OR: Could you please tell me the time?)

2. Ask a desk clerk at a hotel to give you the key to your room.

   ____

3. Ask your teacher to explain the meaning of the word *grateful.*

   ____

4. Ask the cashier at the store to give you change for a dollar.

   ____

5. Ask a stranger on the street to take a picture of you and your friends.

   ____

6. Ask a taxi driver to take you to the airport.

   ____

7. Ask a neighbor to help you with your suitcases.

   ____

8. Ask a salesperson at a store to show you the brown shoes in the window.

   ____

9. Ask the person in front of you at a basketball game to sit down.

   ____

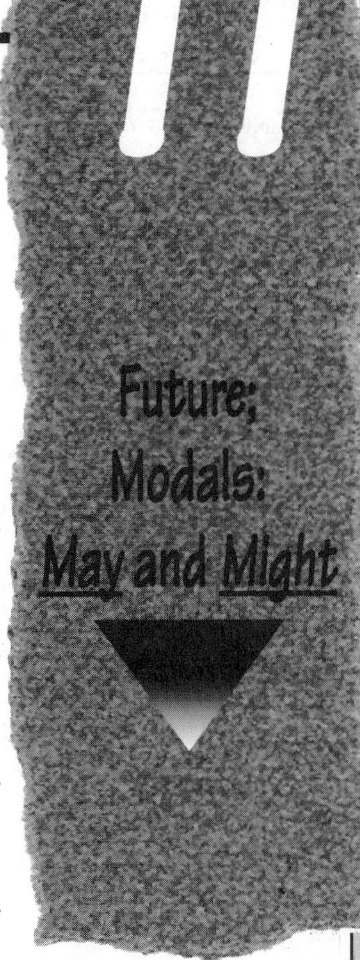

A BE GOING TO FOR THE FUTURE

A.1

Rewrite the sentences. Replace the underlined part with another future time expression. Use **tonight** *or* **next, this,** *or* **tomorrow** *with* **week, month, morning, afternoon, night,** *or* **evening.**

(It's eleven o'clock in the morning on Wednesday, July 3rd.)

1. Keith is going to attend a meeting in four hours.
   Keith is going to attend a meeting this afternoon.
2. Keith and his girlfriend, Andrea, are going to visit a friend in the hospital in eight hours.
   ____
3. Andrea is going to go on vacation in one month.
   ____
4. Keith and his brother are going to play tennis in twenty hours.
   ____
5. Keith's brother is going to see the doctor in one week.
   ____
6. Keith is going to call his mother in eleven hours.
   ____
7. Keith and Andrea are going to go to the movies in thirty-four hours.
   ____

A.2

Rewrite the sentences. Replace the underlined part with another future time expression. Use **in**.

(It is ten o'clock in the morning on Friday, March 5th.)

1. Richard is going to have lunch <u>at two o'clock this afternoon</u>.

   Richard is going to have lunch in four hours.
   ____

2. Richard and Irene are going to see his parents <u>on March 19th</u>.

   ____

3. Irene is going to get a haircut <u>on Monday, March 8th</u>.

   ____

4. Richard is going to graduate from college <u>on May 5th</u>.

   ____

5. Irene is going to arrive at Richard's house <u>at 10:10 this morning</u>.

   ____

A.3

What are your plans for tomorrow? Put a check (✓) next to the things you are probably going to do. Put an **X** *next to the things you are definitely not going to do.*

1. study ______
2. go shopping ______
3. clean ______
4. watch TV ______
5. go out with friends ______
6. listen to music ______
7. visit relatives ______
8. talk on the telephone ______
9. take a shower ______
10. write a letter ______
11. read a newspaper ______
12. stay home ______

A.4

Write six sentences about your plans for tomorrow. Use the information in exercise A.3.

Example: study ✓ write a letter X

I am going to study tomorrow.

I am not going to write a letter.

1. ____________________
2. ____________________
3. ____________________
4. ____________________
5. ____________________
6. ____________________

A.5

Some people are going on vacation. Answer the questions about them. Use **be going to**.

These are some things Nina is taking:
- a guidebook
- a tennis racket
- a bathing suit

These are some things Mr. and Mrs. Wu are taking:
- fishing rods
- bicycles
- paper and envelopes

These are some things Andy is taking:
- a camera
- skis
- books
- a guitar

A. What's Nina going to do on her vacation?

1. *She's going to go sightseeing.*
2. ____________________
3. ____________________

B. What are Mr. and Mrs. Wu going to do on their vacation?

4. ____________________
5. ____________________
6. ____________________

(Continued on next page.)

C. What's Andy going to do on his vacation?

7. ______________________________

8. ______________________________

9. ______________________________

10. ______________________________

A.6

Write sentences about the future. Use **be going to.**

1. It's Wednesday morning. Reggie usually plays tennis on Wednesday afternoon, but he has a bad cold.

   He isn't going to play tennis this afternoon.

2. It's July. Joan usually takes a vacation in August, but she has money problems this year.

   ______________________ a vacation this August.

3. Mary always takes a shower in the morning, but there's no hot water today.

   ______________________ a shower this morning.

4. It's eleven o'clock in the morning. The children usually play outside after lunch, but the weather is terrible today.

   ______________________ outside this afternoon.

5. It's six o'clock. Carl and his wife usually watch television after dinner, but there's nothing good on television.

   ______________________ television tonight.

6. It's eleven o'clock. I usually have lunch around noon, but I finished a big breakfast at 10:30.

   ______________________ lunch at noon today.

7. It's twelve noon. My friend and I like to go swimming on Saturday afternoons, but my friend went away for the weekend and I'm tired.

   ______________________ swimming this afternoon.

8. It's nine o'clock in the morning. Dr. Morita usually sees patients at his office every morning, but there's a serious problem at the hospital. He can't leave until noon.

   ______________________ patients at his office this morning.

9. I usually wake up at six o'clock in the morning, but tomorrow is a holiday.

   ________________________ at six o'clock tomorrow morning.

10. It's ten o'clock in the morning. The letter carrier usually delivers all the mail by one o'clock, but he started late this morning.

    ________________________ all the mail by one o'clock today.

A.7

Write questions. Use **be going to**.

1. What/he/make

   What is he going to make?

2. Who/cook/tonight

   ____

3. When/dinner/be/ready

   ____

4. Why/he/cook/so much food

   ____

5. How long/he/need/to cook the dinner

   ____

6. Who/come

   ____

7. How/he/cook/the lamb

   ____

8. Where/all of your guests/sit

   ____

9. What/you/do

   ____

10. How long/your guests/stay

    ____

A.8

Here are the answers to the questions in exercise A.7. Write each question in the correct blank.

1. **A:** *Who's going to cook tonight?*

   B: My husband.

2. **A:** ______________________________

   B: Soup, salad, lamb, potatoes, some vegetables, and dessert.

3. **A:** ______________________________

   B: We're going to have a dinner party.

4. **A:** ______________________________

   B: He's going to roast it in the oven.

5. **A:** ______________________________

   B: About fifteen of my relatives.

6. **A:** ______________________________

   B: My husband's fast. Probably two or three hours.

7. **A:** ______________________________

   B: I'm going to wash the dishes.

8. **A:** ______________________________

   B: At around seven o'clock.

9. **A:** ______________________________

   B: They're going to come at 6:00 and probably stay until about 11:00.

10. **A:** ______________________________

    B: My sister's going to bring extra chairs.

B PRESENT PROGRESSIVE FOR THE FUTURE

B.1

Underline the verb in each sentence. Write **now** *if the speaker is talking about now. Write* **future** *if the speaker is talking about the future.*

1. What are you doing tomorrow morning? ___future___
2. What are you doing? ___now___
3. I'm doing a grammar exercise. ____________
4. We're not going on vacation in July. ____________
5. She's leaving in two hours. ____________
6. Are you doing anything special? ____________
7. Is the plumber coming soon? ____________
8. The students are not listening. ____________
9. Where are you going? ____________
10. Why is he going to the doctor's office? ____________

B.2

Roger and Helen are taking a trip to Great Britain. Here is their schedule. Write sentences. Use the present progressive.

May 8	6:00 P.M.	Meet your group at the airport
	7:30	Fly to London
May 9	6:45 A.M.	Arrive in London
May 9 and 10		Stay at the London Regency Hotel
May 9	2:00 P.M.	Visit Buckingham Palace
	4:30	Have tea at the Ritz Hotel
	7:30	Go to the theater
May 10	9:00 A.M.	Go on a tour of central London
	12:00 P.M.	Eat lunch at a typical English pub
May 11	8:00 A.M.	Leave for Scotland

1. ___They are meeting their group at the airport at 6:00 P.M. on May 8.___
2. ____________

(Continued on next page.)

3. ______________________________

4. ______________________________

5. ______________________________

6. ______________________________

7. ______________________________

8. ______________________________

9. ______________________________

10. ______________________________

B.3

Write questions. Use the present progressive.

1. you/go/to English class/tomorrow

   Are you going to English class tomorrow?

2. you/go/to the movies/this weekend

   ____

3. you/take a trip/next week

   ____

4. your friend/come over/to your place/in two hours

   ____

5. your classmates from English class/meet you/for lunch tomorrow afternoon

   ____

6. your mother/drive to work/tomorrow

   ____

7. your father/take an English class/next year

   ____

8. your neighbors/make a party/for you/this weekend

   ____

9. you and your friends/play cards/next Saturday

____

10. your parents/have dinner/with your English teacher/the day after tomorrow

____

B.4

Answer the questions in exercise B.3. Use short answers.

1. _______________
2. _______________
3. _______________
4. _______________
5. _______________
6. _______________
7. _______________
8. _______________
9. _______________
10. _______________

B.5

Ask Rosemary about her vacation plans. Write questions. Use a word from each column and the present progressive.

Why When Where Who How long What How	you	stay take go go with leave drive get there

1. *Where are you going?*

   To Colorado.

2. _______________

   On September 16th.

(Continued on next page.)

3. ______________________________

By car.

4. ______________________________

We're going camping.

5. ______________________________

Two weeks.

6. ______________________________

Some friends from college.

7. ______________________________

A tent, sleeping bags, and bikes.

C *WILL* FOR THE FUTURE

C.1

Complete the conversations. Use **I'll** *and the words in the box.*

buy you some	make you a sandwich	wash them
get you some water	close the window	drive you
turn on the air conditioner	get you some aspirin	help you

1. **A:** I'm cold.

   B: *I'll close the window.*

2. **A:** I'm thirsty.

   B: ______________________________

3. **A:** I can't lift this box.

   B: ______________________________

4. **A:** I need some stamps.

   B: ______________________________

5. **A:** I'm hot.

   B: ______________________________

6. **A:** I'm hungry.

   B: ______________________________

7. **A:** I have a headache.

   B: ______________________________

8. **A:** I'm late for class.

   B: ______________________________

9. **A:** There are dirty dishes in the sink.

   B: ______________________________

C.2

Write the sentences in full form.

1. She'll be happy to see you. *She will be happy to see you.*
2. It'll be sunny tomorrow. ______________________________
3. They won't know the story. ______________________________
4. It won't be easy. ______________________________
5. We'll take you to Ottawa. ______________________________
6. I won't stay there for a long time. ______________________________
7. He'll tell you later. ______________________________

C.3

Write the sentences with contractions.

1. We will meet you at 8:00. *We'll meet you at 8:00.*
2. He will not lose his job. ______________________________
3. I will have a cup of coffee. ______________________________
4. It will rain this evening. ______________________________
5. She will not be happy. ______________________________
6. They will have a good time. ______________________________
7. You will not like it. ______________________________

C.4

Complete the sentences. Choose the correct words.

1. **A:** What's the weather forecast for tomorrow?

   B: The newspaper says it ___will snow___.
   a. is snowing
   b. will snow

2. **A:** Where are you going with the soap and water?

   B: I ________________ wash the car.
   a. am going to
   b. will

3. **A:** Do you see my umbrella?

   B: Yes, it's over there. I ________________ get it for you.
   a. am going to
   b. will

4. **A:** Why is Myra so happy these days?

   B: She ________________ get married.
   a. is going to
   b. will

5. **A:** Why ________________ see that film?
   a. are you going to
   b. will you

   B: I heard it was good.

6. **A:** The dishwasher isn't working. I'm going to call the repairman.

   B: No, don't. I ________________ it.
   a. am fixing
   b. will fix

7. **A:** I think men ________________ dresses in the future.
   a. are wearing
   b. will wear

   B: You're crazy!

8. **A:** ____________________ anything this weekend?
   a. Are you doing
   b. Will you do

   B: I'm not sure yet. Why?

9. **A:** ____________________ everything by computer in fifty years?
   a. Are people buying
   b. Will people buy

   B: Maybe.

C.5

Write negative sentences with the same meaning.

1. The car will be small.

   The car won't be big.

2. I'll leave early.

   ____

3. It'll be cold.

   ____

4. Coffee will cost less.

   ____

5. The dishes will be clean.

   ____

6. We will come after seven o'clock.

   ____

7. Mr. and Mrs. McNamara will buy an old car.

   ____

8. I'll make a few eggs.

   ____

9. Valerie will win the game.

   ____

10. The parking lot will be empty.

    ____

C.6

A fortune teller is telling Mark about his future. Complete the conversation. Use **will** *and the words in parentheses.*

Fortune teller: Your future (be) ______________________ a happy one.
1.

Mark: (I/be) ______________________ rich?
2.

Fortune teller: Yes. You (marry) ______________________ a very rich woman.
3.

Mark: Where (I/meet) ______________________ her?
4.

Fortune teller: That I can't tell you, but it (be) ______________________ love at first sight.
5.

Mark: (she/love) ______________________ me forever?
6.

Fortune teller: Forever.

Mark: When (we/meet) ______________________ ?
7.

Fortune teller: Soon.

Mark: What about children?

Fortune teller: You (not have) ______________________ many children—just two, a boy and a girl.
8.

Mark: That's a good number. What else?

Fortune teller: You (be) ______________________ famous.
9.

Mark: Really? Why (I/be) ______________________ famous?
10.

Fortune teller: I'm not sure, but it (not be) ______________________ fun for you.
11.

People (bother) ______________________ you all the time.
12.

Mark: Oh! I (not like) ______________________ that. (our home/have)
13.

______________________ everything?
14.

Fortune teller: Yes, everything.

Mark: Good. Then we (not leave) ______________________ it, and people
15.

(not bother) ______________________ us.
16.

Fortune teller: But then you (become) ______ (17.) a prisoner in your own home. (that/make) ______ (18.) you happy?

Mark: Oh, why isn't life perfect?

Fortune teller: That I cannot tell you.

D MODALS: *MAY* OR *MIGHT* FOR POSSIBILITY

D.1

Write **permission** *if the speaker is giving, refusing, or asking for permission.*
Write **possibility** *if the speaker is talking about possibilities.*

1. Don't call Carol. She may be asleep. *possibility*
2. It's noisy outside. May I close the window? *permission*
3. You may not talk during the test. ______
4. The government may raise taxes. ______
5. Lie down! You might feel better. ______
6. You may enter that room of the museum, but be careful. ______
7. Some of the students might not do the homework. ______
8. May my roommate come to the party, too? ______
9. The mailman is coming. There may be a letter for me. ______
10. Nobody may leave before eleven o'clock. ______

D.2

Rewrite the sentences. Use **may** *or* **might**.

1. Maybe it will snow.

   It may snow. (OR: It might snow.)

2. Perhaps we'll come by taxi.

   ______

3. Perhaps he won't want to come.

   ______

(Continued on next page.)

4. Maybe they'll study.

____

5. Perhaps the store will be closed.

____

6. Maybe she won't finish the work by Friday.

____

7. Maybe the dog will die.

____

8. Perhaps you won't like that kind of food.

____

9. Maybe I won't leave before seven o'clock.

____

10. Perhaps the cookies won't taste good.

____

D.3

Complete the sentences. Use **may** *or* **will**.

1. Tomorrow is my birthday. I ___*will*___ be twenty-five.
2. I'm tall. My children ___*may*___ be tall, too.
3. I don't know anything about that movie. It ______________ not be any good.
4. Are you taking a trip to the United States? You ______________ need a passport. Everybody from Brazil needs one.
5. Don't worry. I ______________ do it. I promise.
6. Ask about the price. The picture ______________ be expensive.
7. The supermarket ______________ sell flowers, but I'm not sure.
8. There's someone at the door. I ______________ open it.
9. The sun ______________ rise tomorrow.
10. The food ______________ be ready. I'm going to look.

D.4

Complete the sentences. Use **may (not)** *or* **might (not)** *and the words in the box.*

bite	close	get lost	have an accident	pass
break	fall	get sick	live	win

1. Janet is worried about her little boy. He's climbing a tree.

   He *may fall (OR: He might fall).*

2. Jimmy has a test today, and he didn't study.

   He ______________________________

3. Lynn is driving fast.

   She ______________________________

4. Wrap those glasses carefully.

   They ______________________________

5. Mark Muller is one of the top tennis players in the world, but he isn't playing well today.

   He ______________________________

6. Don't lose these directions. It's difficult to find my house.

   You ______________________________

7. The woman's injuries are very bad.

   She ______________________________

8. Don't go near that animal.

   It ______________________________

9. Don't go outside with wet hair. It's cold.

   You ______________________________

10. That store never has many customers.

    It ______________________________

UNIT

12

Comparisons

A COMPARATIVE FORM OF ADJECTIVES

A.1

Put a check (✓) next to the statements that are true.

1. Carol is neater than Yoko is.
2. Lulu is older than Pete is.
3. Doug is younger than Carol is.
4. Carol is more hardworking than Norma is.
5. Yoko is more interested in her studies than Carol is.
6. Lulu is busier than Pete is.
7. Yoko is farther from home than Carol is.

A.2

Put the words in the box in the correct column.

big	difficult	heavy	messy
careful	easy	high	noisy
comfortable	expensive	hot	old
crowded	fast	intelligent	pretty
dangerous	friendly	long	small

Words With One Syllable	**Words With Two Syllables**	**Words With Three or Four Syllables**
big	*careful*	*comfortable*

A.3

Complete the sentences. Use the comparative form of the adjectives.

1. That car is old, but this car is *older* .
2. That book is good, but this book is ________ .

3. The train station is far, but the airport is ________________ .

4. The student in the front is intelligent, but the student in the back is ________________ .

5. The service at that restaurant is bad, but the food is ________________ .

6. My sister's messy, but my brother is ________________ .

7. This chair is comfortable, but that chair is ________________ .

8. My husband is careful, but his father is ________________ .

9. The singer is pretty, but the actress is ________________ .

10. Chemistry is difficult, but physics is ________________ .

11. This unit's easy, but the last unit was ________________ .

A.4

Complete the sentences. Use the comparative form of the adjectives in parentheses and **than**.

1. San Francisco is ___*smaller than*___ New York.
(big, small)

2. The Nile River is ____________________ the Mississippi River.
(long, short)

3. A Mercedes is ____________________ a Volkswagen.
(cheap, expensive)

4. Mexico City is ____________________ Rome.
(big, small)

5. The Himalayan Mountains are ____________________ the Rocky Mountains.
(low, high)

6. Egypt is ____________________ Canada.
(cold, hot)

7. Skiing is ____________________ golf.
(safe, dangerous)

8. Cities are ____________________ villages.
(crowded, empty)

(Continued on next page.)

9. Cars are ________________________ bicycles.
(noisy, quiet)

10. A rock is ________________________ a leaf.
(heavy, light)

11. Cheetahs are ________________________ monkeys.
(slow, fast)

12. Dogs are ________________________ wolves.
(friendly, unfriendly)

A.5

Write questions. Use the comparative form of the adjectives.

Example: Carol/neat/or/messy/Yoko
Is Carol neater or messier than Yoko?

1. this unit/easy/or/difficult/the last unit

____

2. this workbook/cheap/or/expensive/the grammar book

____

3. you/young/or/old/your best friend

____

4. you/tall/or/short/your teacher

____

5. your hometown/big/or/small/Los Angeles

____

6. the weather today/good/or/bad/the weather yesterday

____

A.6

Answer the questions in exercise A.5.

Example: (Is Carol neater or messier than Yoko?)

Carol is messier.

1. ______
2. ______
3. ______
4. ______
5. ______
6. ______

B ADVERBS OF MANNER; COMPARATIVE FORM OF ADVERBS

B.1

Write **adjective** *if the underlined word is an adjective. Write* **adverb** *if the underlined word is an adverb.*

1. Norma works <u>hard</u>. *adverb*
2. Carol's room is <u>dirty</u>. *adjective*
3. Pete drives <u>slowly</u>. ______
4. This exercise isn't <u>hard</u>. ______
5. Everyone's going to come <u>early</u>. ______
6. Carol did <u>badly</u> on the test. ______
7. Don't drive <u>fast</u>. ______
8. The food smells <u>good</u>. ______
9. That shirt is <u>ugly</u>. ______
10. I want to speak English <u>fluently</u>. ______

(Continued on next page.)

11. Carry these glasses carefully. ______________________________

12. I was tired yesterday. ______________________________

B.2

Find the ten adverbs in the box.

B	H	A	P	P	I	L	Y	F	X	X	X
A	E	A	S	I	L	Y	Q	A	X	X	X
D	A	N	G	E	R	O	U	S	L	Y	X
L	V	G	X	X	X	X	I	T	X	X	X
Y	I	R	P	A	T	I	E	N	T	L	Y
X	L	I	X	X	X	X	T	X	X	X	X
X	Y	L	X	W	E	L	L	X	X	X	X
X	X	Y	X	X	X	X	Y	X	X	X	X

B.3

Complete the sentences. Use the adverbs in exercise B.2.

1. It's snowing ____heavily____ . We can't drive in this weather.
2. Please play ____________________ . The baby's sleeping.
3. Vinny drives ____________________ . One day he's going to have an accident.
4. Lenore was an hour late for class. Her teacher looked at her ____________________ .
5. The children opened their Christmas presents ____________________ .
6. She plays the guitar very ____________________ . Everyone loves to listen to her.
7. I never eat my father's food. He cooks ____________________ .
8. I can't understand him. He speaks ____________________ .
9. I waited ____________________ , but the doctor never came.
10. I didn't get lost. I found the restaurant ____________________ .

B.4

Complete the sentences. Use the adjectives in the box in some sentences. In other sentences, use the adverb form of an adjective in the box.

angry	easy	loud
beautiful	fast	quiet
careful	good	tired

1. **A:** Shh! Be ___quiet___ ! The baby's sleeping.

   B: Okay. I'll open the door ___quietly___ .

2. **A:** The flowers are ____________________ .

   B: They smell ____________________ , too.

3. **A:** Is Gerry a ____________________ eater?

   B: Yes, she eats very ____________________. She always finishes dinner before me.

4. **A:** You look ____________________ .

   B: I am ____________________. I'm going to bed.

5. **A:** Did Samara do ____________________ on the test?

   B: Yes. She got an A. She's a ____________________ student.

6. **A:** Does your daughter drive ____________________ ?

   B: Oh, yes. She's a very ____________________ driver. I never worry about her.

7. **A:** The music in that apartment is always ____________________ .

   B: You're right. They play their music ____________________ . It's awful.

8. **A:** Why did she leave the room so ____________________ ?

   B: I'm not sure. I think she was ____________________ with her boss.

9. **A:** That was an ____________________ test.

   B: I agree. I answered all the questions very ____________________ .

B.5

Complete the sentences. Use the comparative form of the adverb.

1. **A:** Did Ruben come early?

   B: Yes, but I came *earlier* .

2. **A:** Does Alejandro work hard?

   B: Yes, but En Mi works ____________________ .

3. **A:** Did your team play well?

   B: Yes, but the other team played ____________________ .

4. **A:** Does Andrew type carefully?

   B: Yes, but Brian types ____________________ .

5. **A:** Did the waiter yesterday serve you fast?

   B: Yes, but the waiter last week served us ____________________ .

6. **A:** Does Adam write neatly?

   B: Yes, but his sister writes ____________________ .

7. **A:** Does your husband dance badly?

   B: Yes, but I dance ____________________ .

8. **A:** Does the mechanic on Elm Street fix cars quickly?

   B: Yes, but the mechanic on Diamond Street fixes them ____________________ .

9. **A:** Did you learn to ride a bike easily?

   B: Yes, but my younger brother learned ____________________ .

10. **A:** Can you jump high?

    B: Yes, but Charlie can jump ____________________ .

11. **A:** Did the cashier speak to you rudely?

    B: Yes, but the manager spoke to me ____________________ .

C ADJECTIVE + *ENOUGH*; *TOO* + ADJECTIVE; *VERY* + ADJECTIVE

C.1

Match the questions and answers.

1. __b__ What's wrong with the soup?
2. _____ Do you want to go to that restaurant?
3. _____ Can you hear the music?
4. _____ Why are the other boys playing baseball without you?
5. _____ Do you like boxing?
6. _____ Are you going to wear that dress?
7. _____ Do you drive?
8. _____ Are you happy with your grade on the test?

a. No, it's too violent.
b. It's too salty.
c. I'm not good enough.
d. No, it's too tight.
e. No, I'm not old enough.
f. No, it's too crowded.
g. No, it isn't high enough.
h. No, the radio's not loud enough.

C.2

Rewrite the sentences. Use **too**.

1. The bathing suit isn't dry enough for me to wear.

   The bathing suit is too wet for me to wear.

2. The apartment isn't big enough for six people.

   ____

3. Shirley and Jack aren't fast enough to run in the race.

   ____

4. The car isn't cheap enough for us to buy.

   ____

(Continued on next page.)

5. The children aren't old enough to start school.

____

6. The room isn't warm enough.

____

C.3

Rewrite the sentences. Use **enough**.

1. It's too cold to sit outside.

   It isn't warm enough to sit outside.

2. The jacket is too small for me.

____

3. The break was too short.

____

4. It's too dark to take a picture.

____

5. It's too noisy to talk.

____

6. Buses are too slow.

____

C.4

Complete the sentences. Use **too** *or* **very**.

1. **A:** Do you like my new dress?

   B: Yes, it's ____________________ pretty.

2. **A:** Put these sweaters in the drawer.

   B: I can't. The drawer's ____________________ full.

3. **A:** Mommy, I want to swim in the baby pool.

   B: You're ____________________ big. You're not a baby.

4. **A:** What do you think of that hotel?

   B: The rooms are ____________________ nice, but it's expensive.

5. **A:** How's the weather in Montreal in January?

   B: It's ____________________ cold.

6. **A:** Can you read that sign?

   B: No, it's ____________________ far away.

7. **A:** Are you going to buy the stereo?

   B: I think so. The price is ____________________ good.

8. **A:** The floor's ____________________ dirty.

   B: I'll wash it.

9. **A:** Put this bag in your pocket.

   B: I can't. It's ____________________ big.

C.5

Write one sentence from the two sentences.

1. I can't watch the movie. It's too sad.

   The movie is too sad for me to watch.

2. I can't drink this coffee. It's too strong.

   ____

3. Pete did not understand the instructions. They were too difficult.

   ____

4. We can't eat the fruit. It's not ripe enough.

   ____

5. We can't wait. The line's too long.

   ____

6. She didn't wash the sweater by hand. It was too dirty.

   ____

7. You can't marry him. He's not rich enough.

   ____

8. You can eat the eggs. They're cooked enough.

   ____

C.6

Complete the sentences. Use **enough** *or* **too** *and the adjective in parentheses.*

1. **A:** Why did you take the pants back to the store?

   B: They were (long) ___too long___. I exchanged them for a shorter pair.

2. **A:** Do you want me to wash the car again?

   B: Yes. It's (clean) ___not clean enough___.

3. **A:** Let's go into that big old house. I want to see what's in there.

   B: No, I don't want to. I'm (frightened) ______________________. There may be ghosts.

4. **A:** Are the shoes comfortable?

   B: No, they're (big) ______________________. I need a size 8, and they're a size 7.

5. **A:** Why didn't you get the tickets?

   B: It was (late) ______________________. There weren't any left yet.

6. **A:** Is the soup okay?

   B: Yeah. Now it's (hot) ______________________. Thanks for heating it up.

7. **A:** I'm going to go on a diet.

   B: Why? Are all your clothes (tight) ______________________?

8. **A:** Why do I need to write this composition again?

   B: Because it's (short) ______________________. You wrote only 150 words, and I told you to write at least 250 words.

9. **A:** Can I borrow your bike?

   B: No, I'm sorry, but there's something wrong with the brakes. It's (safe) ______________________ to ride.

10. **A:** Dad, can we go in the water now?

    B: I don't know. It was cold before. Put your toe in the water and see if it's (warm) ______________________ now.

11. **A:** Why aren't the plants in the living room growing?

    B: Probably because it's (sunny) ______________________. They need more light.

D *AS* + ADJECTIVE/ADVERB + *AS*; *THE SAME* + NOUN + *AS*; *THE SAME AS*; *DIFFERENT FROM*

D.1

Put a check (✓) next to the sentences that are true.

1. Canada is the same size as the United States.
2. Lions are not as big as elephants.
3. 32° F is the same as 0° C.
4. The Statue of Liberty in New York is not as old as the Pyramids in Egypt.
5. Alaska is as cold as Antarctica.
6. A whale is different from a fish.
7. The British flag has the same colors as the American flag.
8. Silver is as valuable as gold.

D.2

Complete the sentences. Use **as** *or* **than**.

1. Russia is bigger ___*than*___ the United States.
2. Is your classroom the same size ___*as*___ the other classrooms?
3. South America is not as big ______________ Asia.
4. English is more difficult ______________ my native language.
5. The president of the United States is not the same age ______________ the leader of my country.
6. I'm more tired today ______________ I was yesterday.
7. Are doctors as rich ______________ lawyers?
8. Are you as thin ______________ your best friend?
9. Thelma's the same height ______________ her brother.
10. Are animals more intelligent ______________ human beings?
11. This book is better ______________ that one.
12. Some people are friendlier ______________ others.

D.3

Write sentences. Use the adjective in parentheses and **as . . . as** *or* **more . . . than**. *(Remember:* = *means* **equals**; < *means* **less**; > *means* **more**.*)*

1. a Fiat < a Mercedes (expensive)

   A Fiat isn't as expensive as a Mercedes.

2. the book > the film (interesting)

   The book is more interesting than the film.

3. my apartment = your apartment (big)

   My apartment is as big as your apartment.

4. trains < airplanes (fast)

   ___

5. January = February (cold)

6. the chair = the sofa (comfortable)

7. the governor of Oregon < the president of the United States (famous)

8. the bank < the post office (far)

9. grapefruits = lemons (sour)

10. jazz > rock music (relaxing)

11. chocolate ice cream < vanilla ice cream (good)

12. some people > other people (violent)

13. college < high school (easy)

____

14. these boxes = those boxes (heavy)

____

D.4

Write questions. Use **the same** *and a word in the box.*

age	distance	color	height	length	price	size	weight

1. *Is your sister's hair the same color as your hair?*

   No. My sister's hair is brown. My hair's black.

2. ____

   No. I'm 1.69 meters tall. My brother's 1.78 meters tall.

3. ____

   No. My mother's fifty-nine years old. My father's sixty-two.

4. ____

   No. The dining room's smaller than the living room.

5. ____

   Yes. The apples and the oranges are both sixty cents a pound.

6. ____

   No. I'm thinner than my brother.

7. ____

   No. *War and Peace* is over a thousand pages long. *Crime and Punishment* is much shorter.

8. ____

   No. The subway station is farther than the bus stop.

D.5

Write sentences. Use **the same as** *or* **different from**.

1. a wife and a housewife

   A wife is different from a housewife.

2. the U.S.A. and the United States

   The U.S.A. is the same as the United States.

3. a bike and a bicycle

4. a TV and a television

5. North America and the United States

6. 10,362 and 10.362

7. 3 × 16 and 16 × 3

8. 16 ÷ 3 and 3 ÷ 16

9. \$1 and £1

10. a snack bar and a restaurant

11. 12:00 P.M. and noon

12. a plane and an airplane

E *MORE/LESS/FEWER* + NOUN; COMPARATIVE FORM OF ADJECTIVE + NOUN

E.1

Complete the sentences. Choose the correct word.

1. Alaska has ____________________ snow than Texas.
   a. more
   b. less

2. North America has ____________________ countries than Europe.
   a. more
   b. fewer

3. Small towns have ____________________ traffic than big cities.
   a. more
   b. less

4. There are ____________________ car accidents than train accidents.
   a. more
   b. fewer

5. Young people have ____________________ health problems than old people.
   a. more
   b. fewer

6. Germany has ____________________ oil than Iran.
   a. more
   b. less

7. Deserts have ____________________ rain than jungles.
   a. more
   b. less

8. Honolulu has ____________________ people than New York.
   a. more
   b. fewer

E.2

Write the words in the box in the correct column.

bedrooms	furniture
brothers	homework
cars	hours
children	jewelry
coffee	meat
courses	mistakes
food	money
free time	pairs of shoes
friends	traffic
fruit	women

FEWER	LESS
bedrooms	jewelry

E.3

Write sentences. Use **more . . . than, less . . . than,** *and* **fewer . . . than.**

1. Gail has five friends. Noah has fifteen friends.

   Gail has fewer friends than Noah.

2. Gail doesn't eat much fruit. Noah eats a lot of fruit every day.

   Gail eats less fruit than Noah.

3. Gail has three hours of homework every day. Noah has two hours of homework every day.

   Gail has more homework than Noah.

4. Gail has two brothers. Noah has one brother.

   Gail ______________________________

5. Gail works twenty hours a week. Noah works thirty hours a week.

   Gail ______________________________

6. Gail makes $5.50 an hour. Noah makes $7.15 an hour.

   Gail ______________________________

7. Gail is taking five courses this semester. Noah is taking four courses.

   Gail ______________________________

8. Gail drinks one cup of coffee a day. Noah drinks four cups of coffee a day.

   Gail ______________________________

9. Gail's house has five bedrooms. Noah's house has three bedrooms.

   Gail's house ______________________________

10. Gail has a little free time. Noah has a lot of free time.

    Gail ______________________________

11. Gail has eight pairs of shoes. Noah has ten pairs of shoes.

    Gail ______________________________

12. Gail eats meat once or twice a month. Noah eats meat every day.

    Gail ______________________________

13. Gail's family has three cars. Noah's family has two cars.

    Gail's family ______________________________

14. Gail's brother has two children. Noah's brother has one child.

    Gail's brother ______________________________

15. Gail made two mistakes on last week's test. Noah made eight mistakes.

    Gail ______________________________

E.4

Write sentences.

1. longer/my sister/I/hair/than/have

   I have longer hair than my sister.

2. Joanne/Steve and Harry/student/than/better/a/is

   ____

3. serious/the other two salesmen/Mr. Page/than/makes/more/mistakes

   ____

4. the other ones/is/book/than/a/difficult/this/more

   ____

5. a/kitchen/the apartments on the first floor/has/bigger/the apartment on the second floor/than

   ____

(Continued on next page.)

6. more/secretaries/police officers/than/jobs/dangerous/have

____

7. than/bigger/Spain/India/population/a/has

____

E.5

Compare big cities and small towns. Use words from each column. (Don't forget! Add **a** *where necessary.)*

A big city A small town	usually has	clean air crowded streets exciting night life friendly people large police department serious parking problems slow way of life small public transportation system	a small town a big city

1. *A small town usually has cleaner air than a big city.*
2. _______________
3. _______________
4. _______________
5. _______________
6. _______________
7. _______________
8. _______________

A PAST PROGRESSIVE: AFFIRMATIVE AND NEGATIVE STATEMENTS, *YES/NO* QUESTIONS AND ANSWERS, *WH-* QUESTIONS

A.1

Put a check (✓) next to the sentences that are true.

1. I was sleeping at six o'clock yesterday morning.
2. While I was having dinner last night, the telephone rang.
3. This time last year I was not studying English.
4. I was walking down the street one day last week when I saw a friend.
5. My classmates and I were not taking a test at this time last week.
6. While I was getting dressed yesterday, birds were singing outside my window.
7. My family and I were watching TV at 9:30 last night.
8. While I was doing my homework the other day, I made some mistakes.

A.2

Complete the sentences. Use the words in the box and the past progressive.

buy some groceries	take a shower
cook dinner	talk on the phone
get gas	type
go to school	wait for the bus
study	wait in line

1. I saw Lulu and Bertha at the bus stop.

   They were waiting for the bus.

2. I called Lulu yesterday, but her line was busy.

   ____

(Continued on next page.)

3. I saw Uncle Bob and Aunt Valerie at the Hillside Restaurant.

____

4. I saw Carol and Yoko at the library last night.

____

5. I saw Pete's new secretary in the office.

____

6. I saw Pete at the supermarket.

____

7. When I called Elenore, she was in the bathroom.

____

8. When I arrived at Norma's apartment, she was in the kitchen.

____

9. When I went to the gas station, Milt was there.

____

10. I saw Doug on 82nd Street.

____

A.3

Write affirmative or negative sentences about the picture on page 63. Use the past progressive.

1. When I saw Doug at the fruit store, he (stand) ___*was standing*___ in line.
2. When I saw Doug at the fruit store, he (eat) ___*wasn't eating*___ an apple.
3. When I saw Doug at the fruit store, he (read) ______________ .
4. When I saw Doug at the fruit store, three other people (wait) ______________ in line.
5. When I saw Doug at the fruit store, the other people (stand) ______________ in front of him.
6. When I saw Doug at the fruit store, he (wear) ______________ pants.
7. When I saw Doug at the fruit store, he (hold) ______________ his history book.

8. When I saw Doug at the fruit store, he (buy) ______________________ bananas.

9. When I saw Doug at the fruit store, the other customers (leave) ______________________ .

A.4

Write sentences. Use the past progressive and the simple past in each sentence.

1. When/the teacher/ask/me a question/I/read

   When the teacher asked me a question, I was reading.

2. While/my father/talk/to me/someone/ring/the doorbell

   ____

3. The boys/play/basketball/when/the fight/start

   ____

4. I/swim/when/I/get/a pain in my leg

   ____

5. When/we/see/the accident/we/drive/down Market Street

   ____

6. The doctor/examine/Mrs. May/when/she/scream

   ____

7. While/I/wash/my hair/I/get/some soap in my eyes

   ____

8. Alan/shave/when/he/cut/himself

   ____

9. The train/come/while/we/get/our tickets

   ____

A.5

Write questions. Use the past progressive.

1. **A:** Simon and Barbara have breakfast between 7:00 and 7:30 every morning.

   B: *Were they having breakfast* yesterday morning at 7:15?

   A: I think so.

2. **A:** Simon meets with his salespeople every morning between 9:00 and 9:30.

   B: ______________________________ at 9:20 yesterday morning?

   A: Probably.

3. **A:** Barbara teaches every day between one o'clock and four o'clock.

   B: ______________________________ yesterday at three o'clock?

   A: Of course.

4. **A:** Simon swims every Monday and Wednesday between noon and 12:45.

   B: ______________________________ last Wednesday at 12:30?

   A: Probably.

5. **A:** Barbara practices the piano every morning between 9:00 and 10:00.

   B: ______________________________ at 9:30 yesterday morning?

   A: Almost definitely.

6. **A:** Simon listens to a business report on the radio every afternoon between 4:30 and 5:00.

   B: ______________________________ at 4:45 yesterday afternoon?

   A: I guess so.

7. **A:** Simon and Barbara have dinner between six o'clock and seven o'clock.

   B: ______________________________ at 6:30 yesterday?

   A: Yes.

8. **A:** Simon and Barbara watch the news every evening between 7:00 and 7:30.

   B: ______________________________ yesterday evening at 7:15?

   A: I think so.

9. **A:** Barbara takes a bath every evening between 9:00 and 9:30.

   B: ______________________________ at 9:15 yesterday evening?

   A: Probably.

A.6

Answer the questions. Use the simple past or the past progressive of the verbs in parentheses.

1a. **A:** What were you doing when it started to rain?

B: We (have) ______________________________ a picnic.

1b. **A:** What did you do when it started to rain?

B: We (hurry) ______________________________ to the car.

2a. **A:** What were you doing when the phone rang?

B: I (watch) ______________________________ TV.

2b. **A:** What did you do when the phone rang?

B: I (answer) ______________________________ it.

3a. **A:** What were the children doing when the fire started?

B: They (sleep) ______________________________ .

3b. **A:** What did the children do when the fire started?

B: They (run) ______________________________ out of the house.

4a. **A:** What were you doing when the teacher came in?

B: We (stand) ______________________________ around.

4b. **A:** What did you do when the teacher came in?

B: We (sit) ______________________________ down.

5a. **A:** What was Susan doing when she fell?

B: She (climb) ______________________________ a tree.

5b. **A:** What did Susan do when she fell?

B: She (call) ______________________________ her mother.

6a. **A:** What was your father doing when he burned his hand?

B: He (iron) ______________________________ .

6b. **A:** What did your father do when he burned his hand?

B: He (put) ______________________________ some ice on the burn.

A.7

Write questions. Use the verbs in the box and **how fast, what, when, where, who,** *or* **why**.

do	drive	go	ride	stand	wait

1. **A:** *Where were you standing* ________ when the accident happened?

   B: I was standing on the corner of Buick and 3rd Street.

2. **A:** ________________________?

   B: I was waiting.

3. **A:** ________________________?

   B: I was waiting for the bus.

4. **A:** ________________________?

   B: I was going to the gym.

5. **A:** ________________________?

   B: Because I always go to the gym on Mondays.

6. **A:** ________________________ the red car?

   B: A teenager was driving the red car.

7. **A:** ________________________?

   B: He was going at least 65 miles per hour.

8. **A:** ________________________?

   B: I don't know. Maybe he was driving so fast because the other person in the car was ill.

9. **A:** ________________________ in the car with him?

   B: An older woman. Maybe it was his mother.

B DIRECT AND INDIRECT OBJECTS

B.1

Who probably said each of the sentences? Match the sentences and speakers.

1. __f__ "Please show me your driver's license."
2. ______ "I'll explain the answers to you in the next class."
3. ______ "Would you cash this check for me?"
4. ______ "I can fix the car for you on Wednesday."
5. ______ "Please pass me the salt and pepper."
6. ______ "Sure. I'll lend you my car for the weekend."
7. ______ "I want to buy my mother something for her birthday."
8. ______ "We'll send the information to you right away."
9. ______ "Could you please give me your passport?"

a. an immigration officer
b. a mechanic
c. someone at a restaurant
d. someone at an office
e. a teacher
f. a police officer
g. a bank customer
h. a friend
i. a child

B.2

Write the direct object and indirect object in each sentence in exercise B.1.

	Direct Object	**Indirect Object**
1.	your driver's license	me
2.		
3.		
4.		
5.		
6.		
7.		
8.		
9.		

B.3

Stephen and Margo got married last month. They got many wedding presents. Complete the sentences. Put the direct object before the indirect object. Be sure to use the correct preposition.

Frank	some glasses
Kate	a silver bowl
Tim and June	a TV
Julie	a painting
Mike and Sally	some dishes
Robert	the wedding cake

1. Frank gave some *glasses to Stephen and Margo.*
2. Kate got ____________________
3. Tim and June bought ____________________
4. Julie sent ____________________
5. Mike and Sally gave ____________________
6. Robert made ____________________

B.4

Christmas is coming soon. Here are the presents Bernie is going to give. Complete the sentences. Put the indirect object before the direct object.

Lucy	a sweater
Bob	a CD
Bill	a book
Marge	some earrings
his brother	some pajamas
his cousin	some sunglasses

1. *He's going to give Lucy a sweater.*
2. ____________________
3. ____________________
4. ____________________
5. ____________________
6. ____________________

B.5

Complete the sentences. Use the correct preposition and **it, them, me, him,** *or* **her**.

1. This is Carol's book. Give *it to her.*
2. This is Pete and Elenore's invitation. Send ______
3. These are Bertha's bananas. Give ______
4. Those are my keys. Hand ______
5. Norma wants those flowers. Buy ______
6. Uncle Bob and Aunt Valerie like that picture. Get ______
7. I want fried eggs. Make ______
8. I need the salt. Pass ______
9. Milt can't find his pen. Find ______
10. Bertha and Lulu want to see the newspaper. Show ______

B.6

Write sentences.

1. lent/him/some money/I.

   I lent him some money.

2. to/some money/I/him/lent.

   ______

3. me/pronounce/this/for/you/would?

   ______

4. the women/the man/something/is/to/showing.

   ______

5. them/you/some help/give/can?

   ______

6. you/tell/the answer/him/did?

   ______

7. these cookies/for/got/I/the children.

   ______

(Continued on next page.)

8. all my friends/birthday cards/I/send.

___

9. fixed/me/Sharon/my watch/for.

___

10. to/the ball/me/throw.

___

11. this sentence/us/would/you/to/explain?

___

12. me/he/fifty dollars/owes

___

C TOO/EITHER

C.1

Complete the sentences. Use **too** *or* **either.**

1. **A:** Simone doesn't speak English perfectly.

   B: I don't, ___either___ .

2. **A:** Peter is eighteen years old.

   B: Fidel and Maria are, ___ .

3. **A:** Doctors study for many years.

   B: Dentists do, ___ .

4. **A:** Penny has two cats.

   B: Dana does, ___ .

5. **A:** We don't know the answer to the third question.

   B: I don't, ___ .

6. **A:** Helga can't ski very well.

   B: Paul can't, ______________________ .

7. **A:** John Kennedy died a long time ago.

   B: Martin Luther King did, ______________________ .

8. **A:** The cake won't be ready in half an hour.

   B: The pie won't, ______________________ .

9. **A:** The hamburger wasn't good.

   B: The french fries weren't, ______________________ .

C.2

Complete the sentences.

1. Carol goes to college in Oregon, and Yoko ______does______ , too.
2. Doug's last name is Winston, and Norma's ______________________ , too.
3. Carol didn't clean up her room yesterday, and Doug ______________________ , either.
4. Carol has a lot of friends, and Yoko ______________________ , too.
5. Lulu has an apartment in Florida, and Bertha ______________________ , too.
6. Pete Winston wasn't home last night, and Elenore ______________________ , either.
7. Carol doesn't speak Japanese, and Lulu ______________________ , either.
8. Doug doesn't have a car, and Norma ______________________ , either.
9. Doug isn't a very good student, and Carol ______________________ , either.
10. Carol went to San Francisco for Thanksgiving, and Yoko ______________________ , too.
11. Carol can drive, and Yoko ______________________ , too.
12. Pete won't be late for work tomorrow, and his secretary ______________________ , either.

C.3

Complete the sentences. Use **too** *or* **either**.

Hi! I'm Anne's mother.
I can speak Spanish,
but I can't speak German.
I don't have much free time.

Hi! I'm Anne's father.
I have brown hair.
I drive to work every day.
I didn't go out last weekend.

Hi! I'm Anne's sister.
I'm not married.
I'm going to Hawaii on vacation.
I wasn't born in a hospital.

Hi! I'm Anne's brother.
I took piano lessons
a long time ago.
I don't know how to ski.
I was a good student in college.

1. Anne doesn't know how to ski, *and her brother doesn't, either.*
2. Anne can speak Spanish, *and her mother can, too.*
3. Anne has brown hair, ______
4. Anne took piano lessons a long time ago, ______
5. Anne isn't married, ______
6. Anne didn't go out last weekend, ______
7. Anne was a good student in college, ______
8. Anne is going to Hawaii on vacation, ______
9. Anne wasn't born in a hospital, ______
10. Anne drives to work every day, ______
11. Anne can't speak German, ______
12. Anne doesn't have much free time, ______

D PHRASAL VERBS WITH DIRECT OBJECTS

D.1

Complete the sentences. Use **away, back, down, in, off,** *or* **on.**

1. I was hot, so I took ___*off*___ my sweater.
2. I was cold, so I put ______________ my jacket.
3. I put all the dishes in the dishwasher. Would you turn it ______________ ?
4. Would you turn ______________ the light? I want to go to sleep.
5. Time is up. Please hand ______________ your test papers.
6. The weather is going to be bad tomorrow. Let's put ______________ the picnic until next weekend.
7. The test is going to begin. Put all your books and notes ______________ .
8. These clothes are too small for the baby now. Let's give them ______________ .
9. I'm going to throw ______________ yesterday's newspaper.
10. Can I give your umbrella ______________ to you tomorrow? I need it today.

D.2

Rewrite the sentences in two different ways.

1. Turn on the TV.	*Turn the TV on.*	*Turn it on.*
2. I'll put away the food.	______________	______________
3. I'll turn down the radio.	______________	______________
4. Let's put off the meeting.	______________	______________
5. Please hand out these papers.	______________	______________
6. I threw away the wrong thing.	______________	______________
7. Please take off your shoes.	______________	______________
8. The store will not take back bathing suits.	______________	______________
9. Turn off the engine.	______________	______________
10. Don't put on any makeup.	______________	______________

D.3

Answer the questions. Use a word from each column.

call give look put take throw turn	it them	away back off on up

1. What do you do with your clothes before you go to bed?

   I *take them off.*

2. What do you do when you want to listen to the radio?

   I ______________________________

3. What do you do with your alarm clock when it rings?

   I ______________________________

4. What do you do with sour milk?

   I ______________________________

5. What do you do with a pen after you borrow it?

   I ______________________________

6. What do you do with your shoes before you leave home?

   I ______________________________

7. What do you do with a stereo when it isn't loud enough?

   I ______________________________

8. What do you do with the things on your bed when you want to go to sleep?

   I ______________________________

9. What do you do when you don't know the meaning of a word?

   I ______________________________

10. What do you do when you want to talk to your friends on the phone?

    I ______________________________

E PHRASAL VERBS WITHOUT OBJECTS

E.1

Rewrite the sentences. Replace the underlined words. Use the phrasal verbs in the box.

break down	come in	hang up
catch on	eat out	show up
clear up		

1. Please enter.

   Please come in

2. We like to eat in a restaurant.

3. The weather will get better.

4. Some cars often stop working.

5. The taxi will arrive soon.

6. Don't end the phone conversation.

7. Short skirts will probably become popular again.

E.2

Add **it** *where necessary.*

1. **A:** I can't hear the music.

   B: I'll turn ^*it* up.

2. **A:** Is this my hat?

   B: Yes. Put on.

3. **A:** Why are you walking?

   B: The elevator broke down.

4. **A:** Where's the bus?

   B: It always shows up late on Fridays.

5. **A:** Do you want this box?

   B: No. Throw away.

6. **A:** Is your father still on the phone?

   B: No. He hung up.

7. **A:** Do you want to eat home tonight?

   B: No. Let's eat out.

8. **A:** Are you finished with the iron?

   B: Yes. Could you turn off?

9. **A:** May I come in?

   B: Yes. Please sit down.

10. **A:** Where's your new CD player?

    B: It didn't work right, so I took back.

E.3

Complete the sentences. Use one word from each box.

ate	cleared	sat	stayed
broke	grew	showed	stood
came	hung	shut	woke

down	out
in	up

1. One of the students ___*stood up*___ and left the room.
2. I got the wrong number, so I ____________ .
3. It was cloudy in the morning, but in the afternoon it ____________ .
4. I live in Virginia now, but I ____________ in Kansas. My parents still live there.
5. We ____________ at the table and started to eat.
6. Our car ____________ , so we called the mechanic.

7. I ____________________ late at the party, and there was no food left.

8. I didn't leave work on time because a problem ____________________ .

9. There was no food in the refrigerator, so we ____________________ last night.

10. Don't say, "____________________ ." Say, "Be quiet." It's more polite.

11. I'm tired this morning because I ____________________ late last night.

12. I ____________________ in the middle of the night because I had a bad dream.

UNIT

14

Modals: Should, Had better, Have to, Must; Superlatives

A SHOULD

A.1

Complete the sentences. Use **should** *or* **shouldn't**

1. Children ___*shouldn't*___ play with matches.
2. Children ____________ watch television all day long.
3. Children ____________ listen to their parents.
4. Children ____________ eat a lot of candy.
5. Children ____________ play in the street.
6. Teenagers ____________ pay attention in school.
7. Teenagers ____________ keep their bedrooms neat.
8. Teenagers ____________ stay out all night with their friends.
9. Adults ____________ exercise at least twice a week.
10. Adults ____________ drink ten cups of coffee a day.

A.2

Rewrite the sentences. Use **ought to**.

1. You should go to the dentist twice a year.
   You ought to go to the dentist twice a year.
2. I should visit my grandparents more often.
   ____
3. All passengers should arrive at the airport an hour before their flight.
   ____
4. Carol should study harder.
   ____
5. We should take something to the party.
   ____

A.3

Rewrite the sentences. Use **should**.

1. Carol ought to clean her room more often.
   Carol should clean her room more often.
   ____

2. You ought to cook the meat a little longer.
   ____

3. Lulu ought to be nicer to Elenore.
   ____

4. I ought to learn how to type.
   ____

5. Pete and Elenore ought to move into a smaller apartment.
   ____

A.4

Complete the sentences. Use **should** *or* **shouldn't** *and the words in the box.*

get a haircut	smoke
go to the dentist	study more
leave a tip	touch it
leave early	wash it
look for another one	watch it

1. You don't look very nice. You *should get a haircut.*
2. I don't like my job. I ______________________
3. John often has a bad cough. He ______________________
4. Myra has a toothache. She ______________________
5. The car is dirty. You ______________________
6. The waiter is terrible. We ______________________
7. Doug and Jason aren't doing well in math. They ______________________
8. There's going to be a lot of traffic. We ______________________
9. That movie is very violent. The children ______________________
10. That dog may bite. You ______________________

A.5

Complete the dialogue. Write questions with **should**. *Use* **what, who, when, why, how many**, *or* **where** *and the verbs in parentheses.*

A: Let's have a party.

B: Okay. (have) ___When should we have___ it?
1.

A: Let's have it on March 23rd.

B: (have) ______________________ it then?
2.

A: Because it's Lucy's birthday.

B: Oh, that's right. (invite) ______________________?
3.

A: Probably around twenty-five people.

B: (invite) ______________________?
4.

A: Let's see . . . the neighbors, Lucy's family, the people from the office.

B: (buy) ______________________ ?
5.

A: Well, we'll need drinks, potato chips, and things like that.

B: (cook) ______________________ ?
6.

A: I'll make some lasagna.

B: That sounds good, and I'll make some salad. (get) ______________________ a
7.
birthday cake from?

A: I like the Savoy Bakery's cakes.

B: Okay. Let's order one from there.

A: You know, we don't have enough dishes and glasses for twenty-five people.
(do) ______________________ ?
8.

B: That's no problem. We can get paper plates and cups at the supermarket.

A: You're right. That's a good idea. (send) ______________________ out the
9.
invitations?

B: I'll write them this weekend.

B HAD BETTER

B.1

Match the sentences and situations. Write the sentences in the correct boxes.

1. We'd better take a taxi.
2. We'd better ask for directions.
3. We'd better not stay up late.
4. We'd better make sure everything is locked.
5. We'd better look at a map.
6. We'd better not wait for the bus.
7. We'd better not stay in the sun anymore.
8. We'd better get a good night's sleep.
9. We'd better throw away the food in the refrigerator.
10. We'd better put some cream on our arms and legs.

a. We're lost	b. We're getting red	c. We're going to be late
		We'd better take a taxi.

d. We'll be away for three weeks	e. We have an exam tomorrow

B.2

Don and Amy are going to have a dinner party. Complete the sentences. Use **had better** *or* **had better not** *and the words in the box.*

ask Costas to bring her borrow some from the neighbors get a couple of bottles invite him	let the dog in the house make roast beef rent a video film serve shrimp sit together at the table

1. Alan can't eat meat.

   We *had better not make roast beef.*

2. Marsha and Sophia don't like each other.

   They ____

3. Tonya has a new boyfriend.

   We ____

4. Joan doesn't like fish or seafood.

   We ____

5. Ed drinks only Diet Coke.

   We ____

6. Chris is allergic to animals.

   We ____

7. We don't have enough chairs.

   We ____

8. The children will probably get bored.

   We ____

9. Sandy doesn't drive, and she can't take a bus here.

   We ____

C HAVE TO, DON'T HAVE TO, MUST

C.1

Put a check (✓) next to the sentences that are true.

1. People in my country have to pay taxes.
2. People in my country don't have to vote.
3. Drivers in my country have to have driver's licenses.
4. Students in my country don't have to wear uniforms in high school.
5. Young people in my country don't have to do military service.
6. Women in my country had to obey their husbands many years ago.
7. Children in my country did not have to go to school many years ago.
8. Children in my country had to go to work at a young age many years ago.

C.2

Rewrite the sentences. Use **have to, has to, don't have to, doesn't have to, had to,** *or* **didn't have to**.

1. It's necessary for me to finish this exercise.

   I *have to finish this exercise.*

2. It isn't necessary for me to do the last exercise again.

   I ______________________________

3. It wasn't necessary for Doug to go to school yesterday.

   Doug ______________________________

4. It was necessary for Carol to clean her room yesterday.

   Carol ______________________________

5. It isn't necessary for Yoko to write her parents every week.

   Yoko ______________________________

6. It wasn't necessary for Pete and Elenore to go shopping last week.

   Pete and Elenore ______________________________

(Continued on next page.)

7. It's necessary for my classmates and me to take tests.

   My classmates and I ______________________________

8. It isn't necessary for Pete and Elenore to buy a new car.

   Pete and Elenore ______________________________

9. It's necessary for Lulu to see her doctor today.

   Lulu ______________________________

10. It's necessary for me to check my answers to this exercise.

   I ______________________________

C.3

Complete the sentences. Use **have to** *and* **don't have to** *in each sentence.*

1. Students ___don't have to___ stay in school twelve hours a day, but they ___have to___ study.
2. Teachers ______________ correct papers, but they ______________ wear uniforms.
3. Police officers ______________ speak a foreign language, but they ______________ wear uniforms.
4. Doctors ______________ study for many years, but they ______________ know how to type.
5. Secretaries ______________ work at night, but they ______________ know how to type.
6. Firefighters ______________ work at night, but they ______________ study for many years.
7. Fashion models ______________ work seven days a week, but they ______________ worry about their appearance.
8. Farmers ______________ get up early in the morning, but they ______________ worry about their appearance.

9. Basketball players ______________________ practice regularly, but they ______________________ play a game every day.

10. Accountants ______________________ be good writers, but they ______________________ be good with numbers.

C.4

Complete the sentences. Use **have to, has to, don't have to,** *or* **doesn't have to**.

1. **A:** Is Dan getting up early this morning?

   B: No, he *doesn't have to get up early this morning.* There's no school.

2. **A:** Is Sheila leaving early today?

   B: Yes, she ______________________ She has a dentist appointment.

3. **A:** Are you going food shopping today?

   B: Yes, I ______________________ There's no food in the house.

4. **A:** Are you and your wife coming by taxi?

   B: Yes, we ______________________ Our car isn't working.

5. **A:** Is Barbara staying at the office late today?

   B: No, she ______________________ Her boss is on vacation.

6. **A:** Are the children cleaning up their room?

   B: No, they ______________________ I cleaned it up yesterday.

7. **A:** Is Mary taking some medicine?

   B: Yes, she ______________________ She has a stomach problem.

8. **A:** Are you paying for the tickets?

   B: No, we ______________________ They're free.

9. **A:** Is José going to wear a suit and tie this morning?

   B: Yes, he ______________________ He's going to an important business meeting.

10. **A:** Does Bonnie do housework?

    B: No, she ______________________ She has a maid.

C.5

Write sentences. Use **must** *or* **mustn't** *and the words in the box.*

drive faster than 55 mph enter go more slowly	make a U-turn park in this area pass	stop turn left turn right

1. 

2. 

3. 

4. 

5. 

6. 

7. 

8. 

9. 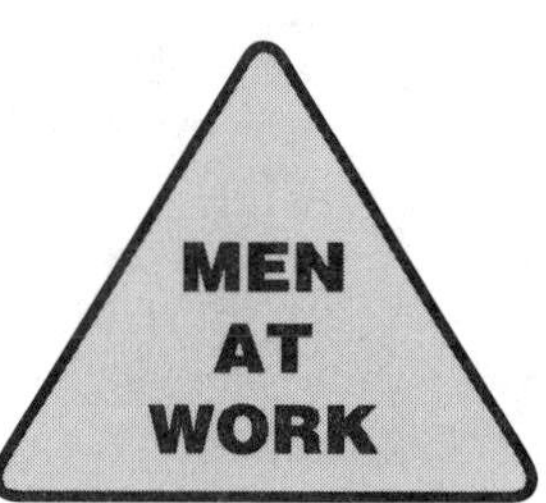

1. *You mustn't enter.*
2. ______________________
3. ______________________
4. ______________________
5. ______________________
6. ______________________
7. ______________________
8. ______________________
9. ______________________

C.6

Mr. and Mrs. Chung were on vacation last week. Write sentences. Use **had to** *or* **didn't have to**.

do anything special find someone to take care of their dog get to the airport on time get up early every morning go to work look for a hotel make the bed every morning pack and unpack suitcases pay their hotel bill wash dishes

1. *They didn't have to do anything special.*
2. ______
3. ______
4. ______
5. ______
6. ______
7. ______
8. ______
9. ______
10. ______

C.7

Write questions.

1. have/English/in class/you/to/do/speak

   Do you have to speak English in class?

2. get up/to/your/have/does/in the morning/at 6:00/mother

   ______

3. you/to/last night/cook/did/have

   ______

(Continued on next page.)

4. best friend/do/does/to/have/your/this exercise

____

5. to/you/on time/in/have/English class/do/be

____

6. friends/learn/to/do/English/your/have

____

7. shave/father/have/your/did/to/yesterday

____

8. your/to work/to/best friend/yesterday/did/have/go

____

9. a/to/test/you/have/did/last week/take

____

C.8

Answer the questions in exercise C.7. Use short answers.

1. (Do you have to speak English in class?)
   Yes, we do.
2. ______________________________
3. ______________________________
4. ______________________________
5. ______________________________
6. ______________________________
7. ______________________________
8. ______________________________
9. ______________________________

C.9

Write questions. Use **have to**.

1. I have to buy some food.

   What *do you have to buy?* ______

2. She has to get a book from the library.

   Why ______

3. He has to go.

   Where ______

4. The teacher had to talk to someone.

   Who ______

5. We had to stay there a long time.

   How long ______

6. The students have to stay after class.

   Why ______

7. I have to use eggs.

   How many eggs ______

8. The high school students had to send their college applications.

   When ______

9. I have to get up early.

   What time ______

10. He had to borrow some money.

    How much money ______

D SUPERLATIVE FORM OF ADJECTIVES AND ADVERBS

D.1

Answer the questions about the Winston family. Write **Carol, Doug**, *or* **Norma**.

1. Who's the oldest? ___Norma___
2. Who's the youngest? ______
3. Who's the neatest? ______
4. Who lives the farthest from home? ______
5. Who's the most serious of the three? ______
6. Who has the busiest social life? ______
7. Who's most interested in fashionable clothes? ______

D.2

Complete the sentences. Use the superlative form of the adjective.

1. The kitchen is always hot. It's ___the hottest___ room in the house.
2. Roger's a bad student. He's ______ student in the class.
3. Chemistry is hard. For me, it's ______ subject in school.
4. Roses are beautiful flowers. In fact, many people think that roses are ______ flowers.
5. Noon is a busy time at the bank. In fact, it's ______ time.
6. "Married Young" is a funny program. It's ______ program on TV.
7. *Scully's* is a good restaurant. In fact, it's ______ restaurant in town.
8. I think monkeys are ugly. In my opinion, they're ______ animals in the zoo.
9. *Midnight* is a popular nightclub. It's ______ nightclub in town.
10. *Dixon's* has low prices. It has ______ prices in the neighborhood.
11. Pamela's a fast swimmer. She's ______ swimmer on the team.
12. Jake is charming. He's ______ person of all my friends.

D.3

Put the words in the correct order. Then write two sentences. Use the adjectives in parentheses.

1. a train/a plane/a bus (fast)

   A plane is the fastest of the three.

   A train is faster than a bus.

2. a teenager/a child/a baby (old)

3. a Ford/a Rolls Royce/a BMW (expensive)

4. Nigeria / Turkey/Sweden (hot)

5. a street/a path/a highway (wide)

6. a city/a village/a town (big)

7. an elephant/a gorilla /a fox (heavy)

8. an hour/a second/a minute (long)

(Continued on next page.)

9. boxing/golf/soccer (dangerous)

___

___

10. a banana/a carrot/chocolate (fattening)

___

___

D.4

Write sentences. Use the superlative form of the adverbs in parentheses.

1. Andy came at 6:00. Mike came at 6:20. Jean came at 6:40.

   (late) *Jean came the latest.*

   (early) ___

2. The red car is going 50 miles per hour. The blue car is going 65 miles per hour. The white car's going 73 miles per hour.

   (slowly) ___

   (fast) ___

3. Shirley drives well and never has car accidents. Maurice usually drives well, but he had an accident last year. Fran drives badly; she had two accidents last year and one accident this year.

   (dangerously) ___

   (carefully) ___

4. Gary works two miles from his home. Viv works fifteen miles from her home. Harris works thirty miles from his home.

   (close) ___

   (far) ___

5. Milton speaks a few words of Spanish. Linda can speak Spanish, but she always makes mistakes. Carolyn speaks Spanish and never makes mistakes.

   (well) ___

   (badly) ___

6. Sam types fifty words a minute but always makes at least six mistakes. Joan types sixty words a minute but doesn't usually make any mistakes. Renée types seventy-five words a minute but often makes two or three mistakes.

   (quickly) ______________________________

   (accurately) ______________________________

Putting It All Together

A.1

Find the fourteen verb tense mistakes in the postcard. Then correct them.

May 22nd

Dear Mom and Dad,

Greetings from Venice. Dan and I ~~am~~ are fine. We have a wonderful time on our honeymoon. The weather isn't great, but Venice be such a romantic place. It have so many beautiful places.

Yesterday we walk all around the city. We visit several churches. They was so wonderful, and we see so many gorgeous paintings.

Today it rained all morning, so we didn't went far from our hotel. This afternoon we have lunch at a very good restaurant across from the hotel. We both eat special Venetian dishes and enjoyed them very much.

It is five o'clock now, and Dan rests. Tonight after dinner—maybe we'll go to a pizzeria—we take a gondola ride. I can't wait!

Love,

Carol

TO: Pete and Elenore Winston
4526 Riverside Drive
New York, NY 10027

A.2

Read Carol's diary. Then write questions. Use **who, where, when, what, what time, how long,** *or* **why**.

May 20th

Venice is such a wonderful place. We arrived at eleven o'clock this morning, and I already love it. I still can't believe it, but we took a boat from the airport to our hotel on the Grand Canal. Tonight we're going to take a gondola ride.

1. *When did they arrive in Venice?*

   At eleven o'clock on May 20th.

2. ______________________________

   It's on the Grand Canal.

3. ______________________________

   They're going to take a gondola ride.

May 21st

Well, it rained all night last night, so we stayed in our hotel. I really wanted to go on the gondola ride, but it was impossible in the rain.

Today we're going on a walking tour of the city. The tour will start at 9:00. (It's 7:30 now, and Dan is sleeping.) The tour guide is a professor of art history at the university here. I think it will be interesting.

In the evening we're going to have dinner at a restaurant near Piazza San Marco with two people from Canada. We met them yesterday on the boat ride from the airport. Their names are Paul and Myra, and they're going to stay in Venice for two weeks.

4. ______________________________

Because it rained all night.

5. ______________________________

On a walking tour of the city.

6. ______________________________

At 9:00.

7. ______________________________

He's sleeping.

8. ______________________________

A professor of art history.

9. ______________________________

At a restaurant near Piazza San Marco.

10. ______________________________

With two people from Canada.

11. ______________________________

Yesterday.

(Continued on next page.)

12. ______________________________

Paul and Myra.

13. ______________________________

For two weeks.

May 22nd

Dinner was great. Paul is a little strange, but I like Myra a lot. Paul and Dan ate too much. Dan was sick all night and didn't fall asleep until five in the morning. It's already 8:30, and he's still sleeping. Dan loves to sleep. (I didn't know that before the wedding. It's okay. I love him anyway!)

14. ______________________________

Myra.

15. ______________________________

He ate too much.

16. ______________________________

He loves to sleep.

A.3

How will Carol and Dan's life change after marriage? Complete the sentences. Choose the best answers.

1. Carol and Dan __________ find a place to live.
   a. may
   b. have to

2. Dan __________ go out with other women.
   a. mustn't
   b. doesn't have to

3. Carol and Dan __________ buy a house.
   a. may
   b. must

4. Carol and Dan __________________ have a lot of children.
   a. might
   b. have to

5. Carol __________________ fight a lot with Dan.
   a. can't
   b. shouldn't

6. Carol and Dan __________________ be honest with each other.
   a. can
   b. should

7. Carol and Dan __________________ earn money.
   a. may
   b. have to

8. Carol's parents __________________ say bad things about Dan.
   a. don't have to
   b. shouldn't

9. Carol and Dan __________________ help each other with problems.
   a. ought to
   b. mustn't

10. Carol and Dan __________________ listen to Carol's parents.
    a. can't
    b. don't have to

11. Carol __________________ be rude to Dan's family.
    a. mustn't
    b. doesn't have to

12. Carol __________________ ask permission to get married.
    a. couldn't
    b. didn't have to

B.1

Yoko had teacher A this year and teacher B last year. She liked teacher A more. Here are the reasons. Compare the two teachers. Write sentences.

Teacher A	**Teacher B**
1. Teacher A is very patient.	Teacher B isn't very patient.
2. Teacher A is organized.	Teacher B isn't organized.
3. Teacher A is nice.	Teacher B isn't very nice.
4. Teacher A teaches well.	Teacher B doesn't teach well.
5. Teacher A speaks clearly.	Teacher B doesn't speak clearly.
6. Teacher A is friendly.	Teacher B isn't very friendly.
7. Teacher A gives back homework quickly.	Teacher B doesn't give back homework quickly.
8. Teacher A explains things slowly.	Teacher B doesn't explain things slowly.
9. Teacher A gives a little homework.	Teacher B gives a lot of homework.
10. Teacher A rarely makes mistakes.	Teacher B often makes mistakes.
11. Teacher A's class has a relaxed atmosphere.	Teacher B's class doesn't have a relaxed atmosphere.
12. Teacher A gives easy homework.	Teacher B gives difficult homework.
13. Teacher A uses interesting books.	Teacher B doesn't use very interesting books.
14. Teacher A gives long breaks.	Teacher B doesn't give long breaks.
15. Unfortunately, teacher A gives hard tests.	Teacher B doesn't give hard tests.

1. *Teacher A is more patient than teacher B.*
2. ____________________
3. ____________________
4. ____________________
5. ____________________
6. ____________________
7. ____________________
8. ____________________
9. ____________________
10. ____________________
11. ____________________
12. ____________________
13. ____________________
14. ____________________
15. ____________________

B.2

Rewrite the first eight sentences in exercise B.1. Compare teacher B and teacher A.

1. *Teacher B isn't as patient as teacher A.*
2. ______
3. ______
4. ______
5. ______
6. ______
7. ______
8. ______

B.3

Find the ten differences between the pictures. Write sentences on the next page. Use **a few, a little,** *or* **a lot of.**

(Continued on next page.)

1. *There are a few dishes in the first picture, but there are a lot of dishes in the second picture.*

2. ______________________________

3. ______________________________

4. ______________________________

5. ______________________________

6. ______________________________

7. ______________________________

8. ______________________________

9. ______________________________

10. ______________________________

B.4

Write questions about the first picture on page 223. Use **many** *or* **much** *and the words in the box. Then answer the questions.*

dishes	chairs	flowers	glasses
bread	cheese	fruit	orange juice
butter	chocolate	gifts	potato chips

1. *Are there many dishes?*

No, there aren't.

2. ______________________________

____

3. ______________________________

____

4. ______________________________

____

5. ______________________________

____

6. ______________________________

____

7. ______________________________

____

8. ______________________________

____

9. ______________________________

____

10. ______________________________

____

11. ______________________________

____

12. ______________________________

____

UNIT 1 Present Tense of Be

ANSWER KEY

Where the full form is given, the contraction is also acceptable. Where the contracted form is given, the full form is also acceptable.

A.1

2. We are **3.** She is **4.** He is **5.** They are **6.** I am **7.** It is **8.** They are **9.** She is **10.** You are

A.2

2. We **3.** She **4.** It **5.** He **6.** It **7.** They **8.** We **9.** They **10.** He **11.** He **12.** It

A.3

Sentences with: I am/My best friend is/My mother is/My father is/My teacher is/My parents are/My classmates are

B.1

2. We are here. That is wonderful. **3.** Your food is on the table. Good! I am hungry. **4.** Charlie is in love with Linda. But she is married. **5.** I am sorry about the window. That is okay. **6.** I think the picture is beautiful. You are crazy. It is terrible. **7.** I am so glad to be here. We are glad, too.

B.2

2. That woman's beautiful. She's my wife. **3.** Hello. I'm Nancy Marks. Hi. My name's Hank Stewart. **4.** They're nice people. But they're so boring. **5.** My daughter's in the hospital. We're sorry to hear that. **6.** We're glad to meet you. It's nice to meet you, too. **7.** My boyfriend's fifty-five years old. But you're only twenty.

C.1

✓ = 2, 4, 9
3. The people are not in the house. **5.** The dog is not black. **6.** The man is not fat. **7.** The women are not sisters. **8.** It is not cold. **10.** I am not in the picture.

C.2

2. California is not a country. It is a state. **3.** Russia is not small. It is big. **4.** Egypt and China are not people. They are countries. **5.** Boston and New York are not in Canada. They are in the United States. **6.** Miami is not a state. It is a city. **7.** Toronto is not in the United States. It is in Canada. **8.** Toyotas and Fords are not airplanes. They are cars. **9.** New York is not the capital of the United States. Washington, D.C., is the capital of the United States. **10.** Cigarettes are not good for people. They are bad for people. **11.** The sun and the moon are not near Earth. They are far from Earth.

C.3

2. is **3.** is not **4.** are not **5.** are **6.** are not **7.** is **8.** is not **9.** are **10.** is not

C.4

2. I am right. No, you are not. You are wrong. **3.** Mrs. Morris is not well. I know. Her daughter is worried about her. **4.** It is time for bed. But I am not tired. **5.** They are my books. No, they are not. They are my books. **6.** My keys are not here. They are in my bag. **7.** Maria and Ali are not in class today. They are lucky.

C.5

2. I'm afraid. Why? The dog's not dangerous. **3.** The taxi's here. But I'm not ready. **4.** You're not (*or* You aren't) from the hospital. No, we're police officers. **5.** They're not (*or* They aren't) bad children. No, but they're bad students. **6.** You bag's on the table. It's not (*or* It isn't) my bag. **7.** This gift's for you. But it's not (*or* it isn't) my birthday.

D.1

1. Are you Rocky? **2.** Are you and your classmates worried? **3.** Is your teacher in school today? **4.** We are very good students. **5.** I am very thirsty. **6.** Is the dog hungry? **7.** Oregon is near Canada. **8.** Are the children afraid of the dog? **9.** Is your car red? **10.** This exercise is easy.

D.2

2. f **3.** h **4.** j **5.** l **6.** c **7.** g **8.** k **9.** i **10.** e **11.** a **12.** b

D.3

2. Are you happy? **3.** Is your mother a student? **4.** Is your bedroom clean? **5.** Are your friends from Texas? **6.** Is Carol Winston your friend? **7.** Are you a detective? **8.** Is your teacher friendly? **9.** Are your mother and father Canadian? **10.** Are you in love? **11.** Are your classmates middle aged?

D.4

(Probable answers) **2.** Yes, I am. (*or* No, I' m not.) **3.** No, she isn't. **4.** Yes, it is. (*or* No, it isn't.) **5.** No, they're not. **6.** No, she isn't. **7.** No, I'm not. **8.** Yes, she/he is. (*or* No, she/he isn't.) **9.** No, they aren't. (*or* No, they're not.) **10.** Yes, I am. (*or* No, I'm, not.) **11.** No, they're not (*or* they aren't).

E.1

2. It's a quarter after (*or* past) five. It's five-fifteen. **3.** It's five to two in the afternoon. It's one fifty-five in the afternoon. **4.** It's ten o'clock. **5.** It's half past eight. It's eight-thirty. **6.** It's a quarter to two in the afternoon. It's one forty-five in the afternoon. **7.** It's ten to eight in the evening. It's seven-fifty in the evening. **8.** It's twenty-five after (*or* past) eleven at night. It's eleven twenty-five at night. **9.** It's twenty to twelve at night. It's eleven-forty at night. **10.** It's twenty after (*or* past) six in the evening. It's six-twenty in the evening. **11.** It's five after (*or* past) eleven at night. It's eleven oh-five at night. **12.** It's twenty-five to five in the morning. It's four thirty-five in the morning. **13.** It's ten after (*or* past) two in the afternoon. It's two-ten.

Nouns, Adjectives, and Prepositions

A.1

2. a **3.** f **4.** i **5.** g **6.** d **7.** c **8.** b **9.** h

A.2

2. Dustin Hoffman is an actor. **3.** Elizabeth II is a queen. **4.** Madonna is a singer. **5.** Neil Armstrong is an astronaut. **6.** Mikhail Gorbachev is a former political leader. **7.** Yo Yo Ma is a musician. **8.** Kristi Yamaguchi is an ice skater. **9.** Jodie Foster is an actress.

A.3

/z/ dictionaries, girls, lemons, sons; /ɪz/ boxes, classes, houses, watches; /s/ roommates, states, students

A.4

2. women **3.** men **4.** songs **5.** cities **6.** rivers **7.** continents **8.** states **9.** countries **10.** provinces **11.** universities **12.** watches **13.** actresses **14.** mountains

A.5

2. 2 children, 3 children **3.** 6 teeth, 7 teeth **4.** 1 foot, 4 feet **5.** 1 grandchild, 7 grandchildren **6.** 1 person, 9 people **7.** 2 sisters-in-law, 3 sisters-in-law

A.6

3. It's an oven. **4.** It's a house. **5.** They're books. **6.** It's an orange. **7.** They're eyes. **8.** They're boxes. **9.** It's a potato. **10.** It's an egg. **11.** They're apples. **12.** It's a watch.

B.1

2. big **3.** boring **4.** fat **5.** expensive **6.** dirty **7.** noisy **8.** bad **9.** new **10.** cold

B.2

2. They are honest men. **3.** They are tall girls. **4.** They are intelligent animals. **5.** Those books are expensive. **6.** Eggs are white or brown. **7.** They are good actors. **8.** These watches are cheap. **9.** They are interesting stories.

B.3

2. It is a great book. **3.** Bill Clinton is a famous politician. **4.** She is a beautiful singer. **5.** They are intelligent students. **6.** He is a nice man. **7.** They are expensive cameras. **8.** It is a long story. **9.** We are good doctors. **10.** You are a lucky woman.

C.1

2. e **3.** a **4.** b **5.** f **6.** i **7.** g **8.** h **9.** d

C.2

2. your, their **3.** her, his **4.** our, their **5.** my, her **6.** your, his, my (*or* our), Her

C.3

2. He, His **3.** She, her **4.** They, Their, their, It **5.** We, Our **6.** I, my **7.** He, His **8.** We, Our, Its, It **9.** Their, They, They, She

D.1

2. people **3.** map **4.** books **5.** ice cream cone **6.** girlfriend **7.** cats **8.** flowers **9.** exercise **10.** pencils

D.2

2. This is a gift for you. **3.** This hamburger is terrible. These potatoes are awful, too. **4.** This television is heavy. This bookcase is heavy, too. **5.** Brenda, this is Tim. **6.** These shoes are only $35. **7.** This is a great party. **8.** These are beautiful earrings. This bracelet is nice, too. **9.** These cookies are for you. **10.** These are my parents.

D.3

2. What's this? **3.** What's this? **4.** What's this? **5.** What are these? **6.** What are these? **7.** What's this? **8.** What are these? **9.** What are these? **10.** What's this?

E.1

E.2

2. between **3.** next to (*or* near) **4.** near **5.** in **6.** near **7.** between **8.** in **9.** far from **10.** next to (*or* near) **11.** near

UNIT 3 Wh- Questions, Possessive Nouns, Prepositions of Time and Place

A.1

3. Who **4.** Where **5.** Where **6.** What **7.** Who **8.** Where **9.** Who **10.** What **11.** Where **12.** What

A.2

3. What sports are you good at? **4.** Where are they from? **5.** Who is the woman in your garden? **6.** Where is Dallas? **7.** Where are my shoes? **8.** What is in the bag? **9.** Where is the post office? **10.** Who is your favorite writer? **11.** Who are two famous presidents of the United States? **12.** What is that in the tree?

A.3

3. What sports are you good at? Soccer and basketball. **4.** Where are they from? Venezuela. **5.** Who is the woman in your garden? My best friend. **6.** Where is Dallas? In Texas. **7.** Where are my shoes? Under the bed. **8.** What is in the bag? A sandwich. **9.** Where is the post office? On Park Street. **10.** Who is your favorite writer? Shakespeare. **11.** Who are two famous presidents of the United States? Abraham Lincoln and John Kennedy. **12.** What is that in the tree? A bird.

A.4

2. What **3.** What **4.** Who **5.** What **6.** Who **7.** Where

A.5

2. Where's the hospital? **3.** Where are my keys? **4.** Where's Room 203? **5.** Who's Bill Cosby? **6.** Who are Mikhail Gorbachev and Ronald Reagan? **7.** Who are the people in front of the building? **8.** What are Cadillacs? **9.** What's that (*or* this)? **10.** Where's the wastepaper basket?

B.1

3. His last name is Barba. **4.** He's a grandfather. **5.** They are with their grandfather. **6.** Their names are Lydia and Daphne. **7.** She's twelve years old. **8.** Her hair is long. **9.** His dogs are always outside. **10.** He's with his dogs. **11.** Her eyes are blue. **12.** She's afraid of the dogs. **13.** Their food is in the garage. **14.** They are in the garage. **15.** Their friends are not with them today. **16.** They are happy to be with their grandfather.

B.2

3. Whose eggs are they? **4.** Whose bananas are they? **5.** Whose bread is it? **6.** Whose potatoes are they? **7.** Whose cake is it? **8.** Whose milk is it? **9.** Whose orange juice is it? **10.** Whose potato chips are they? **11.** Whose carrots are they? **12.** Whose bag is it?

B.3

1. Winston's **2.** men's **3.** husband's **4.** babies' **5.** girls' school **6.** brothers' **7.** son's **8.** doctor's **9.** teacher's **10.** teachers'

B.4

2. Mrs. Simpson's **3.** Mary Rose's **4.** Nora's **5.** Bill's **6.** Joe Mott's **7.** Dr. Lin's **8.** Maria Lico's **9.** Tom Cho's

C.1

At—night; half past six

In—the morning; the summer; the evening; 1888; May; the spring

On—June 30th; December 3rd; September 15, 1993; Thursday

C.2

2. It's at 2:30. **3.** It's at nine o'clock in the morning. **4.** It's on Friday. **5.** It's on Saturday. **6.** It's at eight o'clock. **7.** No, it's in the afternoon. **8.** It's at three o'clock. **9.** No, it's in the evening.

C.3

2. what day is it? **3.** what is the date (*or* what day is it?) **4.** what time is it? **5.** when is it? **6.** when is it? **7.** what time is it? (*or* when is it?) **8.** when is it open? **9.** when is your birthday? (*or* what day is your birthday?)

D.1

3. 9th **4.** 12th **5.** 23rd **6.** 51st **7.** 72nd **8.** 80th **9.** 95th **10.** 101st **11.** 116th **12.** 200th

D.2

3. third **4.** eleventh **5.** fifteenth **6.** twentieth **7.** thirty-first **8.** forty-seventh **9.** sixty-sixth **10.** eighty-second **11.** ninety-ninth **12.** one hundred and third

D.3

1. Twenty-third Street and First Avenue **2.** Forty-third Street and Tenth Avenue **3.** Fifty-second Street and Sixth Avenue **4.** Eighty-sixth Street and Fifth Avenue **5.** Fourteenth Street and Eighth Avenue **6.** Sixty-ninth Street and Second Avenue

D.4

2. It's on February second. **3.** It's on January thirty-first. **4.** It's on January tenth. **5.** It's on February fifth. **6.** It's on January twentieth. **7.** It's on February ninth. **8.** It's on January third. **9.** It's on February eighteenth. **10.** It's on January first. **11.** It's on February twenty-second.

UNIT 4 Imperatives; There is, There are

A.1

2. e **3.** b **4.** c **5.** a **6.** i **7.** g **8.** j **9.** f **10.** h

A.2

3. Clean **4.** Don't talk **5.** Don't buy **6.** Ask **7.** Don't be **8.** Don't tell **9.** Study **10.** Give **11.** Don't use

A.3

2. Get off **3.** Go (*or* Walk) **4.** turn **5.** Walk (*or* Go) **6.** make **7.** Ring

A.4

2. b **3.** b **4.** a **5.** a **6.** a **7.** b **8.** a **9.** a **10.** b

A.5

2. Let's get something to eat. **3.** Let's go swimming. **4.** Let's go inside. **5.** Let's go out and look for him. **6.** Let's not invite her to the party. **7.** Let's leave.

B.1

2. his daughter **3.** page 104 **4.** the teacher **5.** my ice cream **6.** five stamps

B.2

2. you 3. me **4.** it **5.** her **6.** us **7.** them **8.** him

B.3

1. me **2.** you **3.** his **4.** she, her **5.** its, it **6.** we, us **7.** their, them

B.4

2. you **3.** him **4.** her **5.** me **6.** him **7.** us **8.** them **9.** them **10.** her **11.** her **12.** you

B.5

2. She loves him. **3.** They love us. **4.** We love them. **5.** Tell me the answer. **6.** Show her the paper. **7.** Take them some flowers. **8.** Send me a postcard.

B.6

2. It, it **3.** she, her **4.** him, He **5.** I, me **6.** they, them **7.** we, us **8.** you

C.1

2. There is **3.** there are **4.** There is **5.** there are **6.** There are **7.** there is **8.** There are **9.** There is **10.** there is

C.2

2. There is a knife on the table. **3.** There are two cars in the garage. **4.** There are flowers in the garden. **5.** There is a dog under the bed. **6.** There is a box between the two chairs. **7.** There is a picture on the wall. **8.** There are five books on the floor. **9.** There are seven rooms in this house.

C.3

3. There is a clock in the tree. **4.** There is a bicycle in the tree. **5.** There is a bed in the tree. **6.** There are televisions in the tree. **7.** There are balls in the tree. **8.** There are hats in the tree. **9.** There are books in the tree. **10.** There are cups in the tree. **11.** There are keys in the tree. **12.** There are pens in the tree. **13.** There are eggs in the tree.

C.4

3. There are two beds in every room. **4.** There are two closets in every room. **5.** There isn't a telephone in every room. **6.** There is a television in every room. **7.** There is an air conditioner in every room. **8.** There isn't a refrigerator in every room. **9.** There isn't a swimming pool at the hotel. **10.** There are two restaurants at the hotel. **11.** There are four tennis courts at the hotel. **12.** There aren't tourist shops at the hotel. **13.** There are two parking lots at the hotel.

C.5

3. There are two banks. They are on Main Street. **4.** There are three clothing stores. They aren't very expensive. **5.** There aren't any bookstores. **6.** There are four drugstores. They're small. **7.** There are three gas stations. They are in the center of town. **8.** There aren't any hospitals. **9.** There aren't any movie theaters. **10.** There are two restaurants. They are open for lunch and dinner. **11.** There are three schools. They aren't far from Main Street. **12.** There are two supermarkets. They are big. **13.** There aren't any swimming pools.

D.1

2. a **3.** a **4.** b **5.** b **6.** a **7.** a **8.** b **9.** a

D.2

3. There aren't any students from Russia. **4.** There are many students from Japan. **5.** There are many students from Venezuela. **6.** There is a student from Turkey. **7.** There aren't any students from Morocco. **8.** There is a student from Greece. **9.** There are a few students from Mexico. **10.** There aren't any students from Indonesia. **11.** There are a few students from China. **12.** There aren't any students from France.

E.1

2. Yes, there are. **3.** Yes, there are. **4.** No, there aren't. **5.** No, there aren't. **6.** No, there aren't. **7.** Yes, there are. **8.** No, there aren't. **9.** No, there aren't.

E.2

2. Are there many elephants in India? Yes, there are. **3.** Is there a desert in Canada? No, there isn't. **4.** Are there camels in Saudi Arabia? Yes, there are. **5.** Is there a long river in the Sahara Desert? No, there isn't. **6.** Are there many lions in Russia? No, there aren't. **7.** Are there mountains in Kenya? Yes, there are. **8.** Are there people in the Antarctic? No, there aren't. **9.** Is there a big city in Thailand? Yes, there is. **10.** Is there a monkey in your garden? No, there isn't.

E.3

2. How many telephones (*or* clocks) (*or* bicycles) (*or* beds) are there? **3.** How many balls are there? **4.** How many suitcases are there? **5.** How many hats are there? **6.** How many books are there? **7.** How many cups are there? **8.** How many keys are there? **9.** How many pens are there? **10.** How many eggs are there?

F.1

1. no comma **2.** . . . for you, but it is not . . . **3.** . . . table, and it is big. **4.** no comma **5.** . . . husband, and the jacket . . . **6.** . . . warm, but it is not . . . **7.** . . . beautiful, and it is . . . **8.** no comma

F.2

2. b **3.** a **4.** b **5.** a **6.** b **7.** a **8.** a

F.3

2. d (. . . my family, but I . . .) **3.** b (lot, but there are only . . .) **4.** g (. . . air conditioner, and there is no hot water.) **5.** h (. . . pretty, but they are . . .) **6.** e (. . . big, but they are . . .) **7.** a (. . . good, but it is always . . .) **8.** i (. . . Avenue, and there are . . .) **9.** j (. . . lost, and we are . . .) **10.** f (. . . artist, and we are . . .)

UNIT 5 Present Progressive

A.1

2. e **3.** b **4.** a **5.** c **6.** j **7.** g **8.** f **9.** h **10.** i

A.2

3. getting **4.** shining **5.** rain **6.** make **7.** watching 8. listening **9.** run **10.** hitting **11.** talk **12.** driving **13.** doing **14.** put **15.** begin **16.** studying

A.3

3. I am (*or* I am not) having a good time. **4.** The sun is (*or* is not) shining. **5.** It is (*or* is not) raining. **6.** It is (*or* is not) getting dark. **7.** I am (*or* am not) listening to the radio. **8.** I am (*or* am not) talking on the phone. **9.** I am (*or* am not) sitting on a chair. **10.** My best friend is (*or* is not) sitting next to me. **11.** My neighbors are (*or* are not) making a lot of noise. **12.** I am (*or* am not) writing with a pencil.

A.4

2. is snowing **3.** are skiing **4.** are relaxing **5.** are sitting **6.** is reading **7.** am writing **8.** are making **9.** are enjoying **10.** is playing

B.1

2. Are you wearing glasses? **3.** Is your English teacher correcting papers? **4.** Are you and a friend watching TV? **5.** Are your classmates doing this exercise now? **6.** Are your neighbors having dinner? **7.** Is the sun shining? **8.** Are your friends waiting for you? **9.** Are your parents working? **10.** Are you eating ice cream? **11.** Is your teacher helping you with this exercise? **12.** Are children playing outside?

B.2

2. Yes, I am. (*or* No, I'm not.) **3.** Yes, he/she is. (*or* No, he/she isn't.) **4.** Yes, we are. (*or* No, we aren't.) **5.** Yes, they are. (*or* No, they aren't.) **6.** Yes, they are. (*or* No, they aren't.) **7.** Yes, it is. (*or* No, it isn't.) **8.** Yes, they are. (*or* No, they aren't.) **9.** Yes, they are. (*or* No, they aren't.) **10.** Yes, I am. (*or* No, I'm not.) **11.** Yes, he/she is. (*or* No, he/she isn't.) **12.** Yes, they are. (*or* No, they aren't.)

B.3

2. Is she sleeping? **3.** Are they playing? **4.** Are they swimming? **5.** Is he buying stamps? **6.** Are they having a good time? **7.** Is she visiting someone? **8.** Are they playing tennis? **9.** Is she fixing something? **10.** Is he coming? **11.** Are they waiting for me? **12.** Is he following me?

C.1

2. A pineapple. **3.** They are waiting. **4.** An old woman. **5.** In a store. **6.** A dress. **7.** Behind Doug.

C.2

2. Where are you hiding the gift? **3.** Who is knocking on the door? **4.** What are your children wearing? **5.** Who is she waiting for? **6.** What are you looking for? **7.** Why are they walking to work? **8.** Where are they taking the baby? **9.** Why is she sending him a gift? **10.** What are you doing?

C.3

2. What are you doing? **3.** Why are you leaving so early? **4.** What are you looking for? **5.** Where are you hiding the gift? **6.** Who is knocking on the door? **7.** What are your children wearing? **8.** Who is she waiting for? **9.** Why is she sending him a gift? **10.** Where are they taking the baby?

C.4

2. a **3.** b **4.** a **5.** b **6.** b **7.** a

C.5

2. What are you reading? **3.** What are they eating? **4.** What is he cooking? **5.** Who is coming? **6.** Why are you going to bed? **7.** Where are you going? **8.** Why are you throwing them out? **9.** Where are they swimming? **10.** What are you watching? **11.** Who are they watching? **12.** Who is she dating?

D.1

3. right now **4.** right now **5.** these days **6.** right now **7.** these days **8.** these days **9.** right now **10.** these days

D.2

2. are probably saying **3.** are probably spending **4.** is going **5.** are not making **6.** is getting **7.** is the government doing **8.** Is it doing **9.** are looking **10.** is not giving **11.** are complaining **12.** are writing **13.** are you writing

UNIT 6 Simple Present Tense

A.1

2. They're secretaries. **3.** He's a pilot. **4.** She's a professor. **5.** They're flight attendants. **6.** You're a cook. **7.** You're a salesperson. **8.** She's a doctor.

A.2

2. teaches **3.** sings **4.** dances **5.** plays **6.** manages **7.** collect **8.** paint **9.** washes **10.** fight

A.3

3. doesn't **4.** doesn't **5.** don't **6.** doesn't **7.** don't **8.** don't **9.** don't **10.** don't

A.4

2. take **3.** goes **4.** has **5.** live **6.** don't live **7.** have **8.** don't live **9.** is **10.** lives **11.** has **12.** is **13.** doesn't have **14.** live **15.** studies **16.** works **17.** leaves **18.** doesn't come **19.** isn't **20.** helps **21.** go **22.** don't have **23.** try **24.** don't get

A.5

2. Water doesn't boil at 90° C. It boils at 100° C. **3.** Water doesn't freeze at 5° C. It freezes at 0° C. **4.** The Sun doesn't go around the Earth. The Earth goes around the Sun. **5.** Penguins don't come from the Arctic. They come from the Antarctic. **6.** Cows don't eat meat. They eat grass. **7.** China doesn't have a small population. It has a big population. **8.** Deserts don't have a lot of water. They have a lot of sand. **9.** Elephants don't have small ears. They have big ears. **10.** Egypt doesn't have a cold climate. It has a hot climate. **11.** The sun doesn't shine at night. It shines during the day. **12.** Mice don't run after cats. Cats run after mice.

B.1

2. a **3.** d **4.** a **5.** c **6.** b **7.** d **8.** a **9.** c **10.** b **11.** d **12.** c

B.2

2. f **3.** c **4.** g **5.** b **6.** a **7.** h **8.** d

B.3

3. Yes, she does. **4.** No, she doesn't. **5.** Yes, they do. **6.** Yes, he does. **7.** No, she doesn't. **8.** Yes, he does. **9.** No, they don't. **10.** Yes, they do.

B.4

2. Does your roommate like your girlfriend? **3.** Does the teacher wear glasses? **4.** Does Mr. Flagg have a car? **5.** Do Jack and Jill sleep until ten o'clock? **6.** Does Peter eat fast? **7.** Does she leave for work at the same time every day? **8.** Does the dog eat two times a day? **9.** Does the doctor have your telephone number? **10.** Do football players play in the summer?

B.5

2. Does she have **3.** Do they like **4.** Do you live **5.** Does he know **6.** Do you want **7.** Do you have **8.** Does it belong **9.** Do you like **10.** do you know **11.** Do they work **12.** Does he come

C.1

3. Where **4.** What **5.** Who **6.** What time (*or* When) **7.** Who **8.** Where **9.** When **10.** Why **11.** What time (*or* When) **12.** When

C.2

2. What do you have for breakfast? **3.** What time does your husband get up? **4.** Who corrects your homework? **5.** Where does Rosita work? **6.** When do you and your family go on vacation? **7.** What do you wear to work? **8.** Why do you need more money? **9.** What time do the kids eat lunch? **10.** When does the mail come? **11.** Where does Doug meet his friends? **12.** Who does Milt visit on Sundays?

C.3

2. Orange juice and cereal. **3.** At 6:00 in the morning. **4.** My teacher. **5.** At City Central Bank. **6.** In August. **7.** A suit and tie. **8.** Because I want to buy a sweatshirt. **9.** At noon. **10.** In the morning. **11.** At his school. **12.** His parents.

C.4

2. What time (*or* When) **3.** Who **4.** Where **5.** What **6.** When **7.** Where **8.** Who **9.** Why **10.** What

C.5

2. Why do you drive your children to school? **3.** What do pilots do? **4.** What time (when) does the bank open? **5.** Who do you love? **6.** Where do your brothers live? **7.** Who (usually) does the shopping? **8.** When do American children start school? **9.** Who lives in the big white house? **10.** What do you do on the weekend? **11.** Who has my keys? **12.** Who does the doctor want to see first?

D.1

2. those **3.** Those **4.** that **5.** that **6.** that **7.** that **8.** those **9.** those **10.** those

D.2

1. this **2.** that **3.** this **4.** this **5.** those **6.** These **7.** those **8.** That **9.** These **10.** that

E.1

2. g **3.** a **4.** h **5.** b **6.** c **7.** f **8.** e

E.2

2. No, I prefer the brown ones. **3.** The one in the corner. **4.** No, only the ones in the refrigerator. **5.** This one is terrible. **6.** No, but there's one about a mile away. **7.** The ones on the kitchen table. **8.** No, but Carla wants one. **9.** The other ones are better. **10.** No, give me the ones over there. **11.** But the one on Fifth Street costs less. **12.** Do you want the gold earrings or the silver ones?

UNIT 7 Simple Present Tense and Present Progressive

A.1

✔ - 3, 4, 7, 8, 9

A.2

3. I rarely practice in the middle of the night. **4.** I seldom fight with customers. **5.** I often drive at night. **6.** I am always careful. **7.** I almost always find the problem with the car. **8.** I never put lemon in milk. **9.** I am bored once in a while. **10.** The hospital is open every day. **11.** I almost never wear a suit and tie to work. **12.** We are frequently away from home for three or four days at a time.

A.3

2. How often does Donna play basketball? She frequently plays basketball. **3.** How often does David swim? He never swims. **4.** How often do Barbara and Ed play basketball? They never play basketball. **5.** How often does Ed jog? He often jogs. **6.** How often does Barbara swim? She swims three times a week. **7.** How often do Barbara and David jog? They rarely jog. **8.** How often do Ed and George swim? They swim once or twice a week. **9.** How often do George and David play basketball? They play basketball almost every day. **10.** How often does George jog? He almost never jogs. **11.** How often do you jog? **12.** How often do you do exercises?

A.4

2. a **3.** b **4.** e **5.** c **6.** f **7.** k **8.** h **9.** l **10.** d **11.** j **12.** g

A.5

2. drives, is driving a bus **3.** fixes cars, is fixing cars **4.** serves food, 's serving food **5.** paint pictures, 're painting pictures **6.** do experiments, 're doing experiments **7.** write articles, 're writing articles **8.** cuts meat, 's cutting meat **9.** counts money, 's counting money **10.** bake bread and cake, 're baking bread and cake **11.** waters plants and flowers, 's watering plants and flowers **12.** feeds animals, 's feeding animals

A.6

1. are you doing **2.** Are you doing **3.** am cutting **4.** Do you prepare **5.** eat **6.** do you have **7.** eat **8.** go **9.** are getting **10.** doesn't go **11.** Do your kids go **12.** don't stay up **13.** get up **14.** are **15.** does your daughter do **16.** Does she watch **17.** practices **18.** is practicing **19.** does she practice **20.** Does she play **21.** are **22.** am working **23.** is **24.** Do you have

B.1

3. don't have, non-action verb **4.** is having, action verb **5.** belongs, non-action verb **6.** need, non-action verb **7.** like, non-action verb **8.** come, action verb **9.** smell, non-action verb **10.** are smelling, action verb **11.** do, action verb **12.** hate, non-action verb **13.** don't know, non-action verb **14.** are running, action verb

B.2

2. a **3.** b **4.** a **5.** a **6.** b **7.** a **8.** b **9.** a **10.** a **11.** a **12.** b **13.** b **14.** a

B.3

1. do you want **2.** don't care **3.** Do you want **4.** is playing **5.** don't know **6.** don't have **7.** is raining **8.** have **9.** don't have **10.** don't need **11.** like **12.** wants **13.** don't think **14.** has **15.** is doing **16.** hear **17.** is talking **18.** is talking **19.** doesn't understand **20.** is getting **21.** do you know **22.** know **23.** don't know

C.1

2. f **3.** b **4.** a **5.** c **6.** g **7.** e

C.2

2. to swim **3.** to help **4.** to talk **5.** to move **6.** to be **7.** to receive **8.** to study **9.** to relax

D.1

3. correct **4.** correct **5.** Please bring me my car. **6.** Where is her car? **7.** correct **8.** correct **9.** We need our car. **10.** Their car is expensive. **11.** correct **12.** Why do you want your car?

D.2

2. Mine **3.** his **4.** ours **5.** Yours **6.** theirs **7.** his **8.** hers **9.** Theirs **10.** ours

D.3

2. my, yours, mine **3.** hers, hers **4.** our, ours **5.** Their, their, theirs **6.** his, his

UNIT 8 Simple Past Tense

A.1

2. i **3.** a **4.** e **5.** g **6.** b **7.** c **8.** f **9.** h

A.2

2. Last **3.** Last **4.** Yesterday **5.** yesterday **6.** yesterday **7.** last

A.3

1. Eric traveled to Poland _____ years ago. **2.** Eric visited his college roommate _____ months ago. **3.** Eric called his parents _____ days ago. **4.** Eric talked to his boss about a raise _____ days ago. **5.** Eric graduated from college _____ years ago. **6.** Eric moved to Georgia _____ months ago. **7.** Eric played tennis _____ days ago. **8.** Eric studied Polish _____ years ago. **9.** Eric's grandfather died _____ months ago.

A.4

2. They played basketball **3.** She washed her clothes **4.** They studied **5.** He worked in his garden **6.** She prepared dinner at 6:00 **7.** Anna talked to her daughter **8.** They traveled to France **9.** The bank closed at 3:00 P.M. **10.** They watched television

A.5

1. washed; didn't wash **2.** invited; didn't invite **3.** cleaned; didn't clean **4.** talked; didn't talk **5.** called; didn't call **6.** watched; didn't watch **7.** returned; didn't return **8.** painted; didn't paint **9.** cooked; didn't cook **10.** studied; didn't study

A.6

1. am sitting **2.** am thinking **3.** think **4.** is shining **5.** are singing **6.** rained **7.** stayed **8.** didn't go **9.** washed **10.** cleaned **11.** played **12.** comes **13.** speak **14.** don't speak **15.** laughs **16.** invited **17.** listened **18.** danced **19.** enjoyed **20.** am cooking **21.** need **22.** don't want **23.** know

B.1

3. *put,* irregular, put **4.** *had,* irregular, have **5.** *brushed,* regular, brush **6.** *left,* irregular, leave **7.** *arrived,* regular, arrive **8.** *began,* irregular, begin **9.** *learned,* regular, learn **10.** *finished,* regular, finish **11.** *met,* irregular, meet **12.** *ate,* irregular, eat **13.** *went,* irregular, go **14.** *stayed,* regular, stay

B.2

2. drank **3.** left **4.** met **5.** spoke **6.** went **7.** stole **8.** found **9.** drove **10.** saw **11.** brought **12.** came

B.3

(Probable answers) **2.** I didn't eat three kilos of oranges for breakfast yesterday morning. **3.** I didn't sleep twenty-one hours yesterday. **4.** I didn't bring a horse to English class two weeks ago. **5.** I didn't go to the moon last month. **6.** I didn't meet the leader of my country last night. **7.** I didn't find $10,000 in a brown paper bag yesterday. **8.** I didn't do this exercise two years ago. **9.** I didn't swim thirty kilometers yesterday. **10.** I didn't speak English perfectly ten years ago.

B.4

1. had **2.** didn't get **3.** got **4.** went **5.** met **6.** went **7.** didn't see **8.** didn't have **9.** closed **10.** ate **11.** took **12.** stayed **13.** looked **14.** bought **15.** didn't buy **16.** came **17.** made **18.** didn't have **19.** drove **20.** saw **21.** invited **22.** didn't eat **23.** watched **24.** didn't leave

C.1

2. Yes, they did. **3.** No, she didn't. **4.** Yes, he did. **5.** Yes, she did. **6.** No, they didn't. **7.** No, he didn't. **8.** No, they didn't. **9.** Yes, he did.

C.2

2. Did you do all the homework? **3.** Did you take a bath this morning? **4.** Did your best friend come over to your house last night? **5.** Did you go to bed early last night? **6.** Did your English teacher teach you new grammar last week? **7.** Did you visit the United States ten years ago? **8.** Did your mother and father get married a long time ago? **9.** Did you watch television last night?

C.3

2. Yes, I did. (*or* No, I didn't.) **3.** Yes, I did. (*or* No, I didn't.) **4.** Yes, he/she did. (*or* No, he/she didn't.) **5.** Yes, I did. (*or* No, I didn't.) **6.** Yes, he/she did. (*or* No, he/she didn't.) **7.** Yes, I did. (*or* No, I didn't.) **8.** Yes, they did. (*or* No, they didn't.) **9.** Yes, I did. (*or* No, I didn't.)

C.4

3. Did you buy food for dinner? **4.** got **5.** Did you meet Glen for lunch? **6.** ate **7.** Did you write a letter to Rena? **8.** mailed **9.** Did you go to the bank? **10.** deposited **11.** Did you return the book to the library? **12.** took **13.** Did you look for a birthday present for Jane? **14.** bought **15.** Did you call the doctor? **16.** said **17.** Did you bake some cookies? **18.** had **19.** Did you pick the children up at 4:00? **20.** forgot

D.1

2. k **3.** d **4.** a **5.** i **6.** b **7.** j **8.** g **9.** c **10.** f

D.2

2. When did a human being walk on the moon for the first time? In 1969. **3.** What did William Shakespeare write? Plays like *Romeo and Juliet.* **4.** Where did the Olympic Games start? In Greece. 5. Why did many people go to California in 1849? They wanted to find gold. **6.** How long did John Kennedy live in the White House? Almost three years. **7.** What did Alfred Hitchcock make? Movies. **8.** Why did the Chinese build the Great Wall? They wanted to keep foreigners out of the country. **9.** How long did World War II last in Europe? About six years. **10.** When did Christopher Columbus discover America? In 1492.

D.3

2. Who gave **3.** Who did you see **4.** Who called? **5.** Who wrote **6.** Who took **7.** Who did she send **8.** Who cleaned **9.** Who did she marry? **10.** Who did they stay

D.4

2. Who did you go with? (*or* Who went with you?) **3.** What time (*or* When) did you leave your home? **4.** What time (*or* When) did the movie start? **5.** Why did you leave your house so early? **6.** Where did you eat? (*or* Where did you have dinner?) **7.** Where did you meet your friend? **8.** What did you eat (*or* have)? **9.** Who saw you? **10.** Why did you talk to the manager? **11.** Where did you go after dinner? **12.** What did you see? **13.** Where did you see the movie?

UNIT 9 Simple Past of *Be*

A.1

3. The shirt was $29.99. **4.** The tie was $16. **5.** The socks were $8. **6.** The sweater was $39. **7.** The coat was $145. **8.** The pajamas were $19.99. **9.** The shirts were $14.99. **10.** The gloves were $25. **11.** The hat was $22. **12.** The shoes were $65.

A.2

3. William Shakespeare and Charles Dickens weren't Canadian. **4.** Ronald Reagan wasn't the first president of the United States. **5.** Charlie Chaplin and Marilyn Monroe were movie stars. **6.** The end of World War I wasn't in 1922. **7.** *E.T.* was the name of a movie. **8.** Toronto and Washington, D.C., weren't big cities 300 years ago. **9.** Indira Gandhi and Napolean were famous people. **10.** Margaret Thatcher was a political leader. **11.** Oregon and Hawaii weren't part of the United States in 1776. **12.** Disneyland wasn't a famous place 100 years ago.

A.3

2. No, they weren't. (*or* Yes, they were.) **3.** Yes, I was. (*or* No, I wasn't.) **4.** Yes, he was. (*or* No, he wasn't.) **5.** Yes, it was. (*or* No, it wasn't.) **6.** Yes, I was. (*or* No, I wasn't.) **9.** Yes, we were. (*or* No, we weren't.) **10.** Yes, I did. (*or* No, I didn't.) **11.** Yes, it was. (*or* No, it wasn't.) **12.** Yes, I did. (*or* No, I didn't.) **13.** Yes, he/she did. (*or* No, he/she didn't.) **14.** Yes I was. (*or* No, I wasn't.) **15.** No, they didn't.

A.4

2. Were they on sale? Yes, they were only $25. **3.** Were you at home last night? No, I was at the library. **4.** Were the guests late for the party? No, they were all on time. **5.** Was it warm in Australia? The weather was beautiful every day. **6.** Was the movie good? It was okay. **7.** Were the people at the party friendly? Most of them were very nice. **8.** Was he there? No, he was at a meeting.

A.5

3. is **4.** is **5.** is **6.** are **7.** is **8.** Is **9.** is **10.** was **11.** was **12.** were **13.** Were **14.** were **15.** were **16.** was **17.** were **18.** were **19.** Are **20.** are

B.1

2. a **3.** a **4.** b **5.** a **6.** a **7.** b **8.** b **9.** b

B.2

1. did **2.** were **3.** did **4.** was **5.** were **6.** did **7.** was **8.** did **9.** was **10.** was **11.** did **12.** were

B.3

2. How was the weather? **3.** How did you get to the beach? **4.** What was the problem with the bus? **5.** Why did you go there? **6.** Who were you with? **7.** Where did your friends meet you? **8.** Why were your friends late? **9.** What did you wear? **10.** Where was your husband? **11.** Why was he angry? **12.** When did he come home?

B.4

2. were you **3.** was it **4.** were they afraid **5.** was the score **6.** was the name of the store **7.** were they born **8.** were they here **9.** were you with **10.** was Eleanor Roosevelt **11.** were your teachers

C.1

✔ - 1, 3, 6, 7, 9

C.2

1. There was **2.** There were **3.** There was **4.** There was **5.** There were **6.** There were **7.** There was **8.** There were **9.** There were **10.** There was

C.3

2. There was, There weren't **3.** There was, There were **4.** There was, There were **5.** There weren't, There was **6.** There was, There were **7.** There was, There weren't **8.** There weren't, There was

C.4

1. Yes, there was. (*or* No, there wasn't.) **2.** Yes, there were. (*or* No, there weren't.) **3.** Yes, there was. (*or* No, there wasn't.) **4.** Yes, there was. (*or* No, there wasn't.) **5.** Yes, there were. (*or* No, there weren't.) **6.** Yes, there were. (*or* No, there weren't.) **7.** Yes, there was. (*or* No, there wasn't.) **8.** Yes, there were. (*or* No, there weren't.)

C.5

2. Was there a view of the sea from your hotel room? **3.** Was there a restaurant in the hotel? **4.** Was there a beach near the hotel? **5.** Were there cheap restaurants? **6.** Were there interesting things to see? **7.** Were there many places to go shopping? **8.** Were there many English-speaking people? **9.** Was there a casino on the island?

UNIT 10 Nouns and Quantifiers; Modals: Can, Could, Would

A.1

2. 5 **3.** 7 **4.** 1 **5.** 9 **6.** 8 **7.** 4 **8.** 1 **9.** 8 **10.** 4 **11.** 5 **12.** 7 **13.** 2 **14.** 8 **15.** 3

A.2

Count Nouns — eggs, vegetables, napkins, bags, potato chips, toothbrushes

Non-count Nouns — ice cream, fruit, milk, rice, food, bread, fish

A.3

Count Nouns — a student, some teeth, some children, some friends, an animal, some people, an uncle, a television, some questions, a computer

Non-count Nouns — some water, some paper, some homework, some advice, some traffic, some furniture, some money, some information, some rain, some oil

A.4

2. a **3.** a **4.** b **5.** a **6.** a **7.** a **8.** b **9.** a **10.** a **11.** b

A.5

3. He bought some orange juice. **4.** He didn't buy any lemons. **5.** He bought a newspaper. **6.** He didn't buy any bread. **7.** He didn't buy any onions. **8.** He didn't buy a toothbrush. **9.** He bought some potatoes. **10.** He didn't buy any lettuce. **11.** He didn't buy any carrots. **12.** He bought some butter. **13.** He bought some milk. **14.** He bought some eggs.

A.6

a lot of/any — food in my refrigerator, money in my pocket, books next to my bed, shirts in my closet, friends, free time, children, work to do today, questions for my teacher, jewelry, medicine in my bathroom, problems with English grammar, photographs in my wallet, ice cream at home

a little/much — cheese in my pocket, food in my refrigerator, money in my pocket, free time, work to do today, jewelry, medicine in my bathroom, ice cream at home

a few/many — books next to my bed, shirts in my closet, friends, children, questions for my teacher, problems with English grammar, photographs in my wallets

B.1

2. d **3.** a **4.** c **5.** g **6.** h **7.** f **8.** e **9.** l **10.** k **11.** j **12.** i

B.2

3. One carton. **4.** Two heads. **5.** Three. **6.** One. **7.** Four rolls. **8.** Three bars. **9.** One tube. **10.** Two.

B.3

4. Is there any furniture in your home? **5.** Are there any clothes in your closet? **6.** Is there any money under your bed? **7.** Is there an alarm clock next to your bed? **8.** Is there any snow on the ground outside your home? **9.** Is there a sink in your bathroom? **10.** Are there any dishes in your kitchen sink? **11.** Are there any pictures on the walls of your bedroom? **12.** Is there any candy in your home? **13.** Is there a window in your kitchen? **14.** Is there a television in your living room?

B.4

1. Yes, there is. (*or* No, there isn't.) **2.** Yes, there are. (*or* No, there aren't.) **3.** Yes, there is. (*or* No, there isn't.) **4.** Yes, there is. (*or* No, there isn't.) **5.** Yes, there are. (*or* No, there aren't.) **6.** Yes, there is. (*or* No, there isn't.) **7.** Yes, there is. (*or* No, there isn't.) **8.** Yes, there is. (*or* No, there isn't.) **9.** Yes, there is. (*or* No, there isn't.) **10.** Yes, there are. (*or* No, there aren't.) **11.** Yes, there are. (*or* No, there aren't.) **12.** Yes, there is. (*or* No, there isn't.) **13.** Yes, there is. (*or* No, there isn't.) **14.** Yes, there is. (*or* No, there isn't.)

B.5

3. How much flour do you need? **4.** How much sugar do you have? **5.** How many bananas do you want? **6.** How many oranges do you want? **7.** How much rice do you need? **8.** How many potatoes do you need? **9.** How much milk do you want? **10.** How many roses do you want? **11.** How many cookies do you have? **12.** How much money do you have?

C.1

2. b **3.** a **4.** b **5.** a **6.** b **7.** b **8.** a **9.** b **10.** a

C.2

2. There are too many days. **3.** There are too many numbers. **4.** There is too much water. **5.** There is too much furniture. **6.** There is too much food. **7.** There are too many birds. **8.** There too much shampoo. **9.** There are not enough batteries. **10.** There is not enough toothpaste. **11.** There is not enough air. **12.** There are not enough chairs.

C.3

3. There were too few people for two teams. **4.** We had too little paper for everyone in the class. **5.** There was too little food for fifteen people. **6.** You have too little information. **7.** There are too many bedrooms in that apartment. **8.** We had too little time for that test. **9.** There are too few bananas for a banana cake. **10.** There are too few sales people at that store.

D.1

2. secretary **3.** driver **4.** summer camp worker

D.2

4. He can drive, and lift 100 pounds. **5.** He can type, and speak Spanish. **6.** She can play the guitar, and draw. **7.** He can't drive, and he can't lift 100 pounds. **8.** She can type, but she can't speak Spanish. **9.** She can lift 100 pounds, but she can't drive. **10.** He can draw, but he can't play the guitar. **11.** She can't draw, and she can't play the guitar. **12.** He can't type, and he can't speak Spanish.

D.3

2. Can your mother lift 100 pounds? **3.** Can your father play the guitar? **4.** Can your best friend ride a horse? **5.** Can your parents speak Spanish? **6.** Can you swim? **7.** Can you type?

D.4

1. Yes, I can. (*or* No, I can't.) **2.** Yes, she can. (*or* No, she can't.) **3.** Yes, he can. (*or* No, he can't.) **4.** Yes, he/she can. (*or* No, he/she can't.) **5.** Yes, they can. (*or* No, they can't.) **6.** Yes, I can. (*or* No, I can't.) **7.** Yes, I can. (*or* No, I can't.)

D.5

2. could practice **3.** couldn't go **4.** couldn't understand **5.** couldn't eat **6.** could play **7.** couldn't find **8.** could hear **9.** couldn't use **10.** could do

D.6

2. Can I (*or* May I) open the window? **3.** Can I (*or* May I) use the telephone? **4.** Can I (*or* May I) give you a ride? **5.** Can I (*or* May I) use (*or* borrow) your eraser? **6.** Can I (*or* May I) have a drink of water? **7.** Can I (*or* May I) ask you a question? **8.** Can I (*or* May I) sit at the empty table in the corner?

E.1

1. At the bus station **2.** On an airplane **3.** At a movie theater

E.2

2. Would you like to have dinner with me? **3.** Sheila would like to talk to you. **4.** Would your parents like to come? **5.** Sandy and Billy would like some coffee. **6.** Would Dan like to come with us? **7.** My friend and I would like a table for two. **8.** Would the teacher like to come to the party? **9.** I would like to take a long trip. **10.** We would like you to have dinner with us.

E.3

2. Ari would like Conchita to bring the CDs. **3.** Ari would like Irene and Amira to help with the cooking. **4.** Ari would like Eric to bring his CD player. **5.** Ari would like Harry, Mike, and Tom to move the furniture. **6.** Ari would like Ellen to buy some ice cream. **7.** Ari would like Victor to pick up the birthday cake. **8.** Ari would like Carmen and Ted to keep Tony busy. **9.** Ari would like Ratana to make the decorations.

E.4

2. Would you like **3.** Would you like **4.** would like **5.** Would you like me to give **6.** What would you like to do **7.** Where would you like to go **8.** Would you like to go **9.** Would you like to see **10.** What time would you like to go **11.** would like to get **12.** Where would you like to eat

E.5

2. Would (*or* Could) you please give me the key to my room? **3.** Would (*or* Could) you please explain the meaning of the word *grateful*? **4.** Would (*or* Could) you please give me change for a dollar? **5.** Would (*or* Could) you please take a picture of me and my friends? **6.** Would (*or* Could) you please take me to the airport? **7.** Would (*or* Could) you please help me with my suitcases **8.** Would (*or* Could) you please show me the brown shoes in the window? Would (*or* Could) you please sit down?

UNIT 11 Future; Modals: May and Might

A.1

2. this evening **3.** next month **4.** tomorrow morning **5.** next week **6.** tonight **7.** tomorrow night

A.2

2. in two weeks **3.** in three days **4.** in two months **5.** in ten minutes

A.3

Answers will vary.

A.4

(Possible answers) I am (*or* am not) going to study. I am (*or* am not) going to go shopping. I am (*or* am not) going to clean. I am (*or* am not) going to watch TV. I am (*or* am not) going to go out with friends. I am (*or* am not) going to listen to music. I am (*or* am not) going to visit relatives. I am (*or* am not) going to talk on the telephone. I am (*or* am not) going to take a shower. I am (*or* am not) going to write a letter. I am (*or* am not) going to read a newspaper. I am (*or* am not) going to stay home.

A.5

2. She's going to play tennis. **3.** She's going to swim. **4.** They're going to fish. **5.** They're going to ride bikes. **6.** They're going to write letters. **7.** He's going to take pictures. **8.** He's going to ski. **9.** He's going to read. **10.** He's going to play the guitar.

A.6

2. She isn't going to take **3.** She isn't going to take **4.** They aren't going to play **5.** They aren't going to watch **6.** I'm not going to have **7.** We're not going to go **8.** He isn't going to see **9.** I'm not going to wake up **10.** He isn't going to deliver

A.7

2. Who is going to cook tonight? **3.** When is dinner going to be ready? **4.** Why is he going to cook so much food? **5.** How long is he going to need to cook the dinner? **6.** Who is going to come? **7.** How is he going to cook the lamb? **8.** Where are all of your guests going to sit? **9.** What are you going to do? **10.** How long are your guests going to stay?

A.8

2. What's he going to make? **3.** Why's he going to cook so much food? **4.** How's he going to cook the lamb? **5.** Who's going to come? **6.** How long's he going to need to cook the dinner? **7.** What're you going to do? **8.** When's dinner going to be ready? **9.** How long are your guests going to stay? **10.** Where're all of your guests going to sit?

B.1

3. <u>am doing</u>, now **4.** <u>are going</u>, future **5.** <u>is leaving</u>, future **6.** <u>Are . . . doing</u>, now **7.** <u>Is . . . coming</u>, future **8.** <u>are . . . listening</u>, now **9.** <u>are . . . going</u>, now **10.** <u>is . . . going</u>, now

B.2

2. They are flying to London at 7:30 on May 8. **3.** They are arriving in London at 6:45 A.M. on May 9. **4.** They are staying at the London Regency Hotel on May 9 and 10. **5.** They are visiting Buckingham Palace at 2 P.M. on May 9. **6.** They are having tea at the Ritz Hotel at 4:30 on May 9. **7.** They are going to the theater at 7:30 on May 9. **8.** They are going on a tour of central London at 9:00 A.M. on May 10. **9.** They are eating lunch at a typical English pub at twelve o'clock on May 10. **10.** They are leaving for Scotland at 8:00 A.M. on May 11.

B.3

2. Are you going to the movies this weekend? **3.** Are you taking a trip next week? **4.** Is your friend coming over to your place in two hours? **5.** Are your classmates from English class meeting you for lunch tomorrow afternoon? **6.** Is your mother driving to work tomorrow? **7.** Is your father taking an English class next year? **8.** Are your neighbors making a party for you this weekend? **9.** Are you and your friends playing cards next Saturday? **10.** Are your parents having dinner with your English teacher the day after tomorrow?

B.4

1. Yes, I am. (*or* No, I'm not.) **2.** Yes, I am. (*or* No, I'm not.) **3.** Yes, I am. (*or* No, I'm not.) **4.** Yes, he/she is. (*or* No, he/she isn't.) **5.** Yes, they are. (*or* No, they aren't.) **6.** Yes, she is. (*or* No, she isn't.) **7.** Yes, he is. (*or* No, he isn't.) **8.** Yes, they are. (*or* No, they aren't.) **9.** Yes, we are. (*or* No, we aren't.) **10.** Yes, they are. (*or* No, they aren't.)

B.5

2. When are you leaving? **3.** How are you getting there? (*or* How are you going?) **4.** Why are you driving? **5.** How long are you staying? **6.** Who are you going with? **7.** What are you taking?

C.1

2. I'll get you some water. **3.** I'll help you. **4.** I'll buy you some. **5.** I'll turn on the air conditioner. **6.** I'll make you a sandwich. **7.** I'll get you some aspirin. **8.** I'll drive you. **9.** I'll wash them.

C.2

2. It will be sunny tomorrow. **3.** They will not know the story. **4.** It will not be easy. **5.** We will take you to Ottawa. **6.** I will not stay there for a long time. **7.** He will tell you later.

C.3

2. He won't lose his job. **3.** I'll have a cup of coffee. **4.** It'll rain this evening. **5.** She won't be happy. **6.** They'll have a good time. **7.** You won't like it.

C.4

2. a **3.** b **4.** a **5.** a **6.** b **7.** b **8.** a **9.** b

C.5

2. I won't leave late. **3.** It won't be hot. **4.** Coffee won't cost more. **5.** The dishes won't be dirty. **6.** We won't come before seven o'clock. **7.** Mr. and Mrs. McNamara won't buy a new car. **8.** I won't make many eggs. **9.** Valeria won't lose the game. **10.** The parking lot won't be full.

C.6

1. will be **2.** Will I be **3.** will marry **4.** will I meet **5.** will be **6.** Will she love **7.** will we meet **8.** won't have **9.** will be **10.** will I be **11.** won't be **12.** will bother **13.** won't like **14.** Will our home have **15.** won't leave **16.** won't bother **17.** will become **18.** Will that make

D.1

3. permission **4.** possibility **5.** possibility **6.** permission **7.** possibility **8.** permission **9.** possibility **10.** permission

D.2

2. We may (*or* might) come by taxi. **3.** He may (*or* might) not want to come. **4.** They may (*or* might) study. **5.** The store may (*or* might) be closed. **6.** She may (*or* might) not finish the work by Friday. **7.** The dog may (*or* might) die. **8.** You may (*or* might) not like that kind of food. **9.** I may (*or* might) not leave before seven o'clock. **10.** The cookies may (*or* might) not taste good.

D.3

3. may **4.** will **5.** will **6.** may **7.** may **8.** will **9.** will **10.** may

D.4

2. may (*or* might) not pass **3.** may (*or* might) have an accident **4.** may (*or* might) break **5.** may (*or* might) not win **6.** may (*or* might) get lost **7.** may (*or* might) not live **8.** may (*or* might) bite **9.** may (*or* might) get sick **10.** may (*or* might) close

UNIT 12 Comparisons

A.1

✓-2, 3, 5, 7

A.2

one syllable — fast, high, hot, long, old, small

two syllables — crowded, easy, friendly, heavy, messy, noisy, pretty

three or four syllables — dangerous, difficult, expensive, intelligent

A.3

2. better **3.** farther **4.** more intelligent **5.** worse **6.** messier **7.** more comfortable **8.** more careful **9.** prettier **10.** more difficult **11.** easier

A.4

2. longer than **3.** more expensive than **4.** bigger than **5.** higher than **6.** hotter than **7.** more dangerous than **8.** more crowded than **9.** noisier than **10.** heavier than **11.** faster than **12.** friendlier than

A.5

1. Is this unit easier or more difficult than the last unit? **2.** Is this workbook cheaper or more expensive than the grammar book? **3.** Are you younger or older than your best friend? **4.** Are you taller or shorter than your teacher? **5.** Is your hometown bigger or smaller than Los Angeles? **6.** Is the weather today better or worse than the weather yesterday?

A.6

1. It is more difficult. (*or* It is easier.) **2.** It is cheaper. **3.** I am younger (*or* I am older.) **4.** I am taller. (*or* I am shorter.) **5.** It is smaller. (*or* It is bigger.) **6.** It is better. (*or* It is worse.)

B.1

3. adverb **4.** adjective **5.** adverb **6.** adverb **7.** adverb **8.** adjective **9.** adjective **10.** adverb **11.** adverb **12.** adjective

B.2

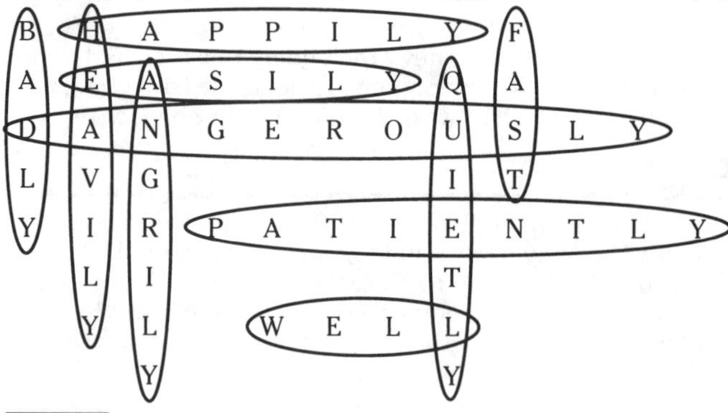

B.3

2. quietly **3.** dangerously **4.** angrily **5.** happily **6.** well **7.** badly **8.** fast **9.** patiently **10.** easily

B.4

2. beautiful, beautiful **3.** fast, fast **4.** tired, tired **5.** well, good **6.** carefully, careful **7.** loud, loudly (*or* loud) **8.** angrily, angry **9.** easy, easily

B.5

2. harder **3.** better **4.** more carefully **5.** faster **6.** more neatly **7.** worse **8.** more quickly **9.** more easily **10.** higher **11.** more rudely

C.1

2. f **3.** h **4.** c **5.** a **6.** d **7.** e **8.** g

C.2

2. The apartment is too small for six people. **3.** Shirley and Jack are too slow to run in the race. **4.** The car is too expensive for us to buy. **5.** The children are too young to start school. **6.** The room is too cold.

C.3

2. The jacket isn't big enough for me. **3.** The break wasn't long enough. **4.** It isn't light enough to take a picture. **5.** It isn't quiet enough to talk. **6.** Buses aren't fast enough.

C.4

1. very **2.** too **3.** too **4.** very **5.** very **6.** too **7.** very **8.** very **9.** too

C.5

2. This coffee is too strong for me to drink. **3.** The instructions were too difficult for Pete to understand. **4.** The fruit is not ripe enough for us to eat. **5.** The line is too long for us to wait. **6.** The sweater was too dirty for her to wash by hand. **7.** He is not rich enough for you to marry. **8.** The eggs are cooked enough for you to eat.

C.6

3. too frightened **4.** not big enough **5.** too late **6.** hot enough **7.** too tight **8.** too short **9.** not safe enough **10.** warm enough **11.** not sunny enough

D.1

✓-2, 3, 4, 6, 7

D.2

3. as **4.** than **5.** as **6.** than **7.** as **8.** as **9.** as **10.** than **11.** than **12.** than

D.3

4. Trains aren't as fast as airplanes. **5.** January is as cold as February. **6.** The chair is as comfortable as the sofa. **7.** The governor of Oregon isn't as famous as the president of the United States. **8.** The bank isn't as far as the post office. **9.** Grapefruits are as sour as lemons. **10.** Jazz is more relaxing than rock music. **11.** Chocolate ice cream isn't as good as vanilla ice cream. **12.** Some people are more violent than other people. **13.** College isn't as easy as high school. **14.** These boxes are as heavy as those boxes.

D.4

2. Are you the same height as your brother? **3.** Is your mother the same age as your father? **4.** Is the dining room the same size as the living room? **5.** Are the apples the same price as the oranges? **6.** Are you the same weight as your brother? **7.** Is *War and Peace* the same length as *Crime and Punishment*? **8.** Is the subway station the same distance as the bus stop?

D.5

3. A bike is the same as a bicycle. **4.** A TV is the same as a television. **5.** North America is different from the United States. **6.** 10,362 is different from 10.362. **7.** 3 x 16 is the same as 16 x 3. **8.** 16 ÷ 3 is different from 3 ÷ 16. **9.** $1 is different from £1. **10.** A snack bar is different from a restaurant. **11.** 12:00 P.M. is the same as noon. **12.** A plane is the same as an airplane.

E.1

1. a **2.** b **3.** b **4.** a **5.** b **6.** b **7.** b **8.** b

E.2

fewer—brothers, cars, children, courses, friends, hours, mistakes, pairs of shoes, women

less—coffee, food, free time, fruit, furniture, homework, meat, money, traffic

E.3

4. has more brothers than Noah **5.** works fewer hours a week than Noah **6.** makes less money an hour than Noah **7.** is taking more courses this semester than Noah **8.** drinks fewer cups of coffee (*or* less coffee) a day than Noah **9.** has more bedrooms than Noah's house **10.** has less free time than Noah **11.** has fewer pairs of shoes than Noah **12.** eats less meat than Noah **13.** has more cars than Noah's family **14.** has more children than Noah's brother **15.** made fewer mistakes on last week's test than Noah

E.4

2. Joanne is a better student than Steve and Harry. **3.** Mr. Page makes more serious mistakes than the other two salesmen. **4.** This is a more difficult book than the other ones. **5.** The apartment on the second floor has a bigger kitchen than the apartments on the first floor. **6.** Police officers have more dangerous jobs than secretaries. **7.** India has a bigger population than Spain.

E.5

2. A big city usually has more crowded streets than a small town. **3.** A big city usually has a more exciting night life than a small town. **4.** A small town usually has friendlier people than a big city. **5.** A big city usually has a larger police department than a small town. **6.** A big city usually has more serious parking problems than a small town. **7.** A small town usually has a slower way of life than a big city. **8.** A small town usually has a smaller public transportation system than a big city.

UNIT 13 Past Progressive; Direct and Indirect Objects

A.1

Answers will vary.

A.2

2. She was talking on the phone. **3.** They were waiting in line. **4.** They were studying. **5.** She was typing. **6.** He was buying some groceries. **7.** She was taking a shower. **8.** She was cooking dinner. **9.** He was getting gas. **10.** He was going to school.

A.3

3. wasn't reading **4.** were waiting **5.** weren't standing **6.** was wearing **7.** wasn't holding **8.** wasn't buying **9.** weren't leaving

A.4

2. While my father was talking to me, someone rang the doorbell. **3.** The boys were playing basketball when the fight started. **4.** I was swimming when I got a pain in the leg. **5.** When we saw the accident, we were driving down Market Street. **6.** The doctor was examining Mrs. May when she screamed. **7.** While I was washing my hair, I got some soap in my eyes. **8.** Alan was shaving when he cut himself. **9.** The train came while we were getting our tickets.

A.5

2. Was he meeting with his salespeople **3.** Was she teaching **4.** Was he swimming **5.** Was she practicing the piano **6.** Was he listening to a business report on the radio **7.** Were they having dinner **8.** Were they watching the news **9.** Was she taking a bath

A.6

1a. were having **1b.** hurried **2a.** was watching **2b.** answered **3a.** were sleeping **3b.** ran **4a.** were standing **4b.** sat **5a.** was climbing **5b.** called **6a.** was ironing **6b.** put

A.7

2. What were you doing? **3.** What were you waiting for? **4.** Where were you going? **5.** Why were you going to the gym? **6.** Who was driving **7.** How fast was he going (*or* driving)? **8.** Why was he driving (*or* going) so fast? **9.** Who was riding

B.1

2. e **3.** g **4.** b **5.** c **6.** h **7.** i **8.** d **9.** a

B.2

2. answers, you **3.** this check, me **4.** the car, you **5.** the salt and pepper, me **6.** my car, you **7.** something, my mother **8.** the information, you **9.** your passport, me

B.3

2. Kate got a silver bowl for Stephen and Margo. **3.** Tim and June bought a TV for Stephen and Margo. **4.** Julie sent a painting to Stephen and Margo. **5.** Mike and Sally gave some dishes to Stephen and Margo. **6.** Robert made the wedding cake for Stephen and Margo.

B.4

2. He's going to give Bob a CD. **3.** He's going to give Bill a book. **4.** He's going to give Marge some earrings. **5.** He's going to give his brother some pajamas. **6.** He's going to give his cousin some sunglasses.

B.5

2. it to them **3.** them to her **4.** them to me **5.** them for her **6.** it for them **7.** them for me **8.** it to me **9.** it for him **10.** it to them

B.6

5. I lent some money to him. **3.** Would you pronounce this for me? **4.** The man is showing something to the women. **5.** Can you give them some help? **6.** Did you tell him the answer? **7.** I got these cookies for the children **8.** I send all my friends birthday cards. **9.** Sharon fixed my watch for me. **10.** Throw the ball to me. **11.** Would you explain this sentence to us? **12.** He owes me fifty dollars.

C.1

2. too **3.** too **4.** too **5.** either **6.** either **7.** too **8.** either **9.** either

C.2

2. is **3.** didn't **4.** does **5.** does **6.** wasn't **7.** doesn't **8.** doesn't **9.** isn't **10.** did **11.** can **12.** won't

C.3

3. and her father does, too **4.** and her brother did, too **5.** and her sister isn't, either. **6.** and her father didn't, either **7.** and her brother was, too **8.** and her sister is, too **9.** and her sister wasn't, either **10.** and her father does, too **11.** and her mother can't, either **12.** and her mother doesn't, either

D.1

2. on **3.** on **4.** off **5.** in **6.** off **7.** away **8.** away **9.** away **10.** back

D.2

2. I'll put the food away. I'll put it away. **3.** I'll turn the radio down. I'll turn it down. **4.** Let's put the meeting off. Let's put it off. **5.** Please hand these papers out. Please hand them out. **6.** I threw the wrong thing away. I threw it away. **7.** Please take your shoes off. Please take them off. **8.** The store will not take bathing suits back. The store will not take them back. **9.** Turn the engine off. Turn it off. **10.** Don't put any makeup on. Don't put it on.

D.3

2. turn it on **3.** turn it off **4.** throw it away **5.** give it back **6.** put them on **7.** turn it up **8.** put them away **9.** look it up **10.** call them up

E.1

2. We like to eat out. **3.** The weather will clear up. **4.** Some cars often break down. **5.** The taxi will show up soon. **6.** Don't hang up. **7.** Short skirts will probably catch on again.

E.2

2. Put it on. **3.** no change **4.** no change **5.** Throw it away. **6.** no change **7.** no change **8.** Could you turn it off? **9.** no change **10.** It didn't work right, so I took it back.

E.3

2. hung up **3.** cleared up **4.** grew up **5.** sat down **6.** broke down **7.** showed up **8.** came up **9.** ate out **10.** shut up **11.** stayed up **12.** woke up

UNIT 14 Modals: *Should*, *Had better*, *Have to*, *Must*; Superlatives

A.1

2. shouldn't **3.** should **4.** shouldn't **5.** shouldn't **6.** should **7.** should **8.** shouldn't **9.** should **10.** shouldn't

A.2

2. I ought to visit my grandparents more often. **3.** All passengers ought to arrive at the airport an hour before their flight. **4.** Carol ought to study harder. **5.** We ought to take something to the party.

A.3

2. You should cook the meat a little longer. **3.** Lulu should be nicer to Elenore. **4.** I should learn how to type. **5.** Pete and Elenore should move into a smaller apartment.

A.4

2. should look for another one. **3.** shouldn't smoke. **4.** should go to the dentist. **5.** should wash it. **6.** shouldn't leave a tip. **7.** should study more. **8.** should leave early. **9.** shouldn't watch it. **10.** shouldn't touch it.

A.5

2. Why should we have **3.** How many (*or* How many people) should we invite? **4.** Who should we invite? **5.** What should we buy? **6.** What should we cook? **7.** Where should we get **8.** What should we do? **9.** When should we send

B.1

a. — We'd better ask for directions. We'd better look at a map.

b. — We'd better not stay in the sun anymore. We'd better put some cream on our arms and legs.

c. — We'd better not wait for the bus.

d. — We'd better make sure everything is locked. We'd better throw away the food in the refrigerator.

e. — We'd better not stay up late. We'd better get a good night's sleep.

B.2

2. had better not sit together at the table. **3.** had better invite him. **4.** had better not serve shrimp. **5.** had better get a couple of bottles. **6.** had better not let the dog in the house. **7.** had better borrow some from the neighbors. **8.** had better rent a video film. **9.** had better ask Costas to bring her.

C.1

Answers will vary.

C.2

2. don't have to do the last exercise again. **3.** didn't have to go to school yesterday. **4.** had to clean her room yesterday. **5.** doesn't have to write her parents every week. **6.** didn't have to go shopping last week. **7.** have to take tests. **8.** don't have to buy a new car. **9.** has to see her doctor today. **10.** have to check my answers to this exercise.

C.3

2. have to; don't have to **3.** don't have to; have to **4.** have to; don't have to **5.** don't have to; have to **6.** have to; don't have to **7.** don't have to; have to **8.** have to; don't have to **9.** have to; don't have to **10.** don't have to; have to

C.4

2. has to leave early today. **3.** have to go food shopping today. **4.** have to come by taxi. **5.** doesn't have to stay at the office late today. **6.** don't have to clean up their room. **7.** has to take some medicine. **8.** don't have to pay for the tickets. **9.** has to wear a suit and tie this morning. **10.** doesn't have to do housework.

C.5

2. You must stop. **3.** You mustn't turn right. **4.** You mustn't turn left. **5.** You mustn't drive faster than 55 mph. **6.** You mustn't park in this area. **7.** You mustn't make a U-turn. **8.** You mustn't pass. **9.** You must go more slowly.

C.6

2. They had to find someone to take care of their dog. **3.** They had to get to the airport on time. **4.** They didn't have to get up early every morning. **5.** They didn't have to go to work. **6.** They had to look for a hotel. **7.** They didn't have to make the bed every morning. **8.** They had to pack and unpack suitcases. **9.** They had to pay their hotel bill. **10.** They didn't have to wash dishes.

C.7

2. Does your mother have to get up at 6:00 in the morning? **3.** Did you have to cook last night? 4. Does your best friend have to do this exercise? **5.** Do you have to be in English class on time? **6.** Do your friends have to learn English? **7.** Did your father have to shave yesterday? **8.** Did your best friend have to go to work yesterday? **9.** Did you have to take a test last week?

C.8

2. Yes, she does. (*or* No, she doesn't.) **3.** Yes, I did. (*or* No, I didn't.) **4.** Yes, he/she does. (*or* No, he/she doesn't.) **5.** Yes, I do. (*or* No, I don't.) **6.** Yes, they do. (*or* No, they don't.) **7.** Yes, he did. (*or* No, he didn't.) **8.** Yes, he/she did. (*or* No, he/she didn't.) **9.** Yes, I did. (*or* No, I didn't.)

C.9

2. does she have to get a book from the library? **3.** does he have to go? **4.** did the teacher have to talk to? **5.** did you have to stay there? **6.** do the students have to stay after class? **7.** do you have to use? **8.** did the high school students have to send their college applications? **9.** do you have to get up? **10.** did he have to borrow?

D.1

2. Doug **3.** Norma **4.** Carol **5.** Norma **6.** Carol **7.** Doug

D.2

2. the worst **3.** the hardest **4.** the most beautiful **5.** the busiest **6.** the funniest **7.** the best **8.** the ugliest **9.** the most popular **10.** the lowest **11.** the fastest **12.** the most charming

D.3

2. A teenager is the oldest of the three. A child is older than a baby. **3.** A Rolls Royce is the most expensive of the three. A BMW is more expensive than a Ford. **4.** Nigeria is the hottest of the three. Turkey is hotter than Sweden. **5.** A highway is the widest of the three. A street is wider than a path. **6.** A city is the biggest of the three. A town is bigger than a village. **7.** An elephant is the heaviest of the three. A gorilla is heavier than a fox. **8.** An hour is the longest of the three. A minute is longer than a second. **9.** Boxing is the most dangerous of the three. Soccer is more dangerous than golf. **10.** Chocolate is the most fattening of the three. A banana is more fattening than a carrot.

D.4

1. Andy came the earliest. **2.** The red car is going the most slowly (*or* slowest). The white car is going the fastest. **3.** Fran drives the most dangerously. Shirley drives the most carefully. **4.** Gary works the closest to his home. Harris works the farthest from his home. **5.** Carolyn speaks Spanish the best. Milton speaks Spanish the worst. **6.** Renée types the most quickly. Joan types the most accurately.

Putting It All Together

A.1

2. We are having a wonderful time on our honeymoon. **3.** . . . Venice is such a romantic place. **4.** It has so many beautiful places. **5.** Yesterday we walked all around the city. **6.** We visited several churches. **7.** They were so wonderful . . . **8.** . . . we saw so many gorgeous paintings. **9.** . . . we didn't go far from our hotel. **10.** This afternoon we had lunch . . . **11.** We both ate special Venetian dishes . . . **12.** . . . Dan is resting **13.** . . . we are going to take a gondola ride.

A.2

2. Where is their hotel? **3.** What are they going to do tonight? **4.** Why did they stay in their hotel last night? **5.** Where are they going today? **6.** What time will the tour start? **7.** What is Dan doing? **8.** Who is the tour guide? **9.** Where are they going to have dinner (in the evening)? **10.** Who are they going to have dinner with? **11.** When did Carol and Dan meet two people from Canada? **12.** What are the two people's names? **13.** How long are Paul and Myra going to stay in Venice? **14.** Who does Carol like a lot? **15.** Why was Dan sick all night? **16.** What does Dan love to do?

A.3

1. b **2.** a **3.** a **4.** a **5.** b **6.** b **7.** b **8.** b **9.** a **10.** b **11.** a **12.** b

B.1

2. Teacher A is more organized than teacher B. **3.** Teacher A is nicer than teacher B. **4.** Teacher A teaches better than teacher B. **5.** Teacher A speaks more clearly than teacher B. **6.** Teacher A is friendlier than teacher B. **7.** Teacher A gives back homework more quickly than teacher B. **8.** Teacher A explains things more slowly than teacher B. **9.** Teacher A gives less homework than teacher B. **10.** Teacher A makes fewer mistakes than teacher B. **11.** Teacher A's class has a more relaxed atmosphere than teacher B's class. **12.** Teacher A gives easier homework than teacher B. **13.** Teacher A uses more interesting books than teacher B. **14.** Teacher A gives longer breaks than teacher B. **15.** Unfortunately, Teacher A gives harder tests than teacher B.

B.2

2. Teacher B isn't as organized as teacher A. **3.** Teacher B isn't as nice as teacher A. **4.** Teacher B doesn't teach as well as teacher A. **5.** Teacher B doesn't speak as clearly as teacher A. **6.** Teacher B isn't as friendly as teacher A. **7.** Teacher B doesn't give back homework as quickly as teacher A. **8.** Teacher B doesn't explain things as slowly as teacher A.

B.3

2. There are a few glasses in the first picture, but there are a lot of glasses in the second picture. **3.** There are a lot of flowers in the first picture, but there are a few flowers in the second picture. **4.** There is a lot of Coke in the first picture, but there is a little Coke in the second picture. **5.** There is a little chocolate in the first picture, but there is a lot of chocolate in the second picture. **6.** There are a few candles on the cake in the first picture, but there are a lot of candles on the cake in the second picture. **7.** There is a lot of fruit in the first picture, but there is a little fruit in the second picture. **8.** There is a lot of cheese in the first picture, but there is a little cheese in the second picture. **9.** There is a little bread in the first picture, but there is a lot of bread in the second picture. **10.** There are a few gifts in the first picture, but there are a lot of gifts in the second picture.

B.4

2. Is there much bread? No, there isn't. **3.** Is there much butter? No, there isn't. **4.** Are there many chairs? Yes, there are. **5.** Is there much cheese? Yes, there is. **6.** Is there much chocolate? No, there isn't. **7.** Are there many flowers? Yes, there are. **8.** Is there much fruit? Yes, there is. **9.** Are there many gifts? No, there aren't. **10.** Are there many glasses? No, there aren't. **11.** Is there much orange juice? Yes, there is. **12.** Are there many potato chips? Yes, there are.